THINK
ABOUT IT
365 Day Devotional

Betty Lambert

ISBN 978-1-0980-1252-6 (paperback)
ISBN 978-1-0980-1253-3 (digital)

Christian Faith Publishing, Inc.
832 Park Avenue
Meadville, PA 16335
www.christianfaithpublishing.com

Printed in the United States of America

DEDICATION

This book is dedicated to Sis Carolyn Davis, who even though she has went on to be with Jesus and her husband, was and continues to be the best spiritual mother anyone could ever hope to have. She never spoke a word of counsel to me without first speaking with God about it. However, it was how she lived her life that became my greatest counsel. To this day she is the godliest woman I have ever met. Without her I would have given up on not only myself but on God as well. She held my hand and prayed me through some very dark times. The life she lived and her faith in God still guide and gives me comfort even through she is no longer here. The title of this book is a phrase she used many times. Every time something truly touched her heart she would say, "Think about it." The scriptures used in this book have made me stop and say, "Think about it." I hope you will take time to stop and think about these scriptures for yourself.

ACKNOWLEDGMENTS

There are several very important people in my life that have inspired, encouraged, prodded, and prayed me through this book.

> My husband Mark, for his love, support and his ability to make me feel like I can move mountains, my pastor, Brandon Davis, for always being willing to reach out and touch God on my behalf and for helping me understand that the only limits I have are the limits I place on myself,
> Sis Tabitha Davis for teaching me the chaos in my life does not have to affect my peace or my joy, and last but not least, four of the greatest and most dedicated prayer warriors in the history of prayer warriors: Lori, Raeanne, Jessica, and Jennie.

Without these people in my life, this book would have never been possible. I love and appreciate you all more than I have words for. Thank you for always having my back, my front, and my sides!

Num. 6:24–26: "The Lord bless you and keep you; the Lord make his face shine on you and be gracious to you; the Lord lift up His countenance on you, and give you peace."

Father, I pray that you bless and keep the person reading this book. Lift them above whatever circumstance they find themselves in. Calm the storms that rage in their lives. Let Your face shine upon them, be gracious in Your pouring out of comfort and peace. Open their eyes and heart to see and feel Your presence in their lives. Open their ears to hear clearly your voice. Bless them abundantly with strength, courage, wisdom, and discernment as they journey down the path You have put them on. Let them feel Your arms around them as You grow their faith through every trial. Fill their hearts and life with true joy. Deliver them from every web the enemy has been able to ensnare them in. Remove every yoke the world and the enemy has put on them. Bind and remove every stronghold he has been able to erect in their life. Father, I pray they find freedom, inspiration, revelation, and many blessings within the pages of this book. In Jesus' name, I pray for this person. I trust Your promises for this person and believe that Your power will free this person to walk in the center of Your perfect will. In Jesus' name, I pray, trust, and believe. Amen.

Thought #1

Isa. 43:18: "Do not…ponder the things of the past."

Understand those things are in your past for a reason. They have no place in your future. Do not continue to think about them or try to carry them into your future. The things of the past will bring certain darkness to the bright future God has planned for you. The past may have helped shape your testimony, but your past is not who you are. Do not let it define you! You are so much more than what you leave behind! Leave the past and all its mistakes where they belong! Keep moving forward with your eyes on God. Let Him take you where you need to be. Let His love define who you are to become.

Phil. 3:13: "Forgetting those things which are behind and reaching forward to those things which are ahead!"

Thought #2

Deut. 6:5–6: "And you must love the Lord your God with all your heart, all your soul, and with all your strength. And you must commit yourselves wholeheartedly to these commands that I am giving you today."

As I sat and meditated on these scriptures, I realize that there are at least two reasons for loving the Lord with all my heart, all my soul, and all my strength. The first and most important one is because my Lord deserves it. He has given me more than I deserve or ever be able to give back. He's loved me more than I'll ever be capable of loving Him. But there is another very good and very practical reason for being wholeheartedly committed to loving the Lord with all your heart, soul, and strength. If we are totally committed to loving Him, then there is no room for anything else. If we are totally, completely, wholeheartedly in love with God, then the enemy of our soul will never be able to find a crack in our armor. If we are consumed with love for the Lord, then we do not have room to love anything else. No worldly idol, no lie, trick, or distraction will be able to take up residence in a temple completely filled with love for the Lover of your heart, mind, and soul. No fiery dart will ever be able to pierce a heart, mind, or soul fully armored with love for God! I encourage you to become fully committed to love, follow, and serve the Lord with your whole heart, mind, and soul. He deserves no less, and neither do you! Protect yourself with love!

Thought #3

Isa. 57:15: "I restore the crushed spirit of the humble and revive the courage of those with repentant hearts."

Aren't you tired of dealing with pain, depression, bitterness, rejection, worry, fear, stress, anger, jealousy? Wouldn't you rather live a life full of joy, instead of this spirit of heaviness that seems to permeate every breath, every thought, and action? Jesus said, "Come." He also says, "Knock and it will be opened, seek and you will find, ask and you will receive." Is it that easy? Yes! Put your life, your heart, and your troubles in His hands. Leave it there, and it becomes His responsibility. He will take that heaviness and those burdens away from you. He will wipe it away like it was never there and He will replace it with more joy than you can imagine. Trust Him, dear friend. Don't you know He is waiting on you? Don't you know He wants to take this from you? He wants to heal your pain and erase your past so that He can give you a future brighter than you can imagine! Trust Him, let Him do this for you!

Thought #4

John 4:13-14: Jesus replied, "Anyone who drinks this water will soon become thirsty again. But those who drink the water I give will never be thirsty again. It becomes a fresh, bubbling spring within them, giving them eternal life."

Once you allow the Lord to fill this old cracked cistern we call our heart, it is our job to become a living, breathing, flowing well of living water. You ever notice what happens to water that just sits in a bucket? It gets slimy, green, dirty, and filled with dead things. But if the water is constantly flowing into the bucket, not only does the water stay fresh, it flows out to water everything around it, giving life to everything it touches. Don't just sit there and let your water become stagnant, green, slimy, and filled with death! What God pours into you, He expects you to pour out to others.

Thought #5

Phil. 4:6–7: "Don't worry about anything: pray about everything; tell God your needs and don't forget to thank Him for His answers. If you do this you will experience God's peace, which is far more wonderful than the human mind can understand."

Have you let your life, your circumstances, your struggles, your storm steal your peace? Or, maybe it was the enemy's tricks and lies that have taken it. Either way, don't fret, stop stressing! The Word says that God has provided an escape! That escape comes through prayer and the blood of Jesus Christ! Whatever it is will torment you no more, if you would just go to God in prayer and believe! I know from experience that the peace God offers is beyond comprehension. Without His hand on my life and the peace He has poured into me, I know without a doubt I would be divorced, addicted to a myriad of drugs and alcohol, or very possibly dead. He has so very graciously brought, or rather carried me through some of the hardest times a parent can face. I want to encourage you to give whatever *it* is to the Lord. Whatever has you at the end of your rope, tied in knots, in total darkness, unable to breathe, God *will* make it better! He can and will end your bondage, if *you* will allow it. He will break every link in the chains that bind you. He will end your torment! Trust Him, have faith in Him; He will take care of you.

Thought #6

Rom. 10:10: "For it is by believing in your heart that you are made right with God, and it is by openly declaring your faith that you are saved."

Once you are saved, you must live as though you are saved. What good does it do to get saved but live, act, talk, and think like the world? For it is by the example of our lives that the world sees God. There is no in between, no gray area. It is simply black or white. If you are saved, then live like it! If we talk the talk, then we must certainly walk the walk. Who are we showing to the world by the example of our life?

Thought #7

Phil. 4:4: "Rejoice in the Lord always."

As Christians, we have no reason to be sad, worried, fretful, angry, embittered, or anxious. If you are an obedient child of the one true living God, then *all* your worries, *all* your battles, *all* your storms have already been handled. Do what you know to do and trust God for the rest. Rejoice in the fact that no matter where you are, He is there with you. Remember and rejoice! Fear and worry or any other lie from the enemy cannot take root in a state of praise, worship, and rejoicing! He is the light at the end of the tunnel. Just keep rejoicing, praising, trusting, and moving toward Him and trust that whatever *it* is, He has already fixed it!

Thought #8

Lam. 3:22–23: "The faithful love of the Lord never ends! His mercies never cease. Great is His faithfulness; His mercies begin fresh every morning."

What an amazing promise! God's love and mercy *never* cease! Every morning you wake up, God's mercies are there, fresh as the morning dew. As faithful as the next day, so is God's love, mercy, grace, and compassion. It never gets old, and it never runs out. Before your eyes even have a chance to open, God is there waiting! What is it you need God to cover for that day? It's there for the taking! You can't need more than God's mercy can cover! If you don't have it, it's because you haven't asked for it. What are you waiting on?

Thought #9

James 1:17: "Every good gift and every perfect gift is from above, and comes down from the Father."

Every good thing you have, every good thing you will ever have comes from God. No one will ever be able to give what God offers! Do not be deceived! What you have did not come by your own hand, by coincidence, or by luck. It was God! Will you accept, or will you throw it back in God's face? Sounds crazy to throw a God-given gift back in God's face, right? But how many times has the ultimate gift of salvation been thrown back in His face? How many times has a gift been refused because it wasn't exactly what we prayed for? How many times has God sent something better than what we asked for and because we didn't recognize it as such, we said, "No, thanks," and persisted in prayer for what *we* thought was best for us? To be honest, it's probably been more times than we would care to know about. Wonder what would happen if we would just learn to trust the only One who truly has our best interests at heart?

Thought #10

Eph. 3:18: "And may you have the power to understand, as all God's people should, how wide, how long, how high, and how deep His love is."

As humans, we do not have the power to understand how wide, long, high, and how deep God's love really is, because we cannot understand true unlimited, unconditional love. It is not in us! But through the help of the blood of Christ, perseverance, time, and spiritual growth, we can begin to see, know, and understand God's love for us. You may say you know, you may say, "My family loves me," or "My 'ride or die' loves me," but could you really stake your life on it? Can you really say that no matter what you did, what you said, or how badly you treated them, they would still love you unconditionally? Would they lay their life down for you? Really? Are you sure? Christ did! If you haven't come to know Christ yet, you haven't felt what true unconditional love is. I encourage you to give your life to Christ and find out what this verse really means.

Thought #11

First Sam. 24:12: "Let the Lord judge between you and me and let the Lord avenge me on you. But my hand shall not be against you."

Whatever has happened, whoever has come against you, whatever has been said or done, you can be assured that God has seen it and has heard it from on high. He will handle it. You won't even have to lift a finger; He's got it! His own Word says, "*No* weapon formed against you shall prosper, and every tongue which rises against you in judgement, you shall condemn." That is the heritage of the servants of the Lord. Resist bitterness and resentment and keep your hands clean. God's got it, and He'll do a better job than you could ever fathom. He is your protector and your shield. Trust Him and His love for you. Wait upon the Lord and expect to see your miracle unfold. I myself can testify to the truth of these verses!

Thought #12

Ezek. 36:26: "And I will give you a new heart, and I will put a new spirit in you. I will take out your stony, stubborn heart and give you a tender, responsive heart."

How awesome is that? God can take the parts of our spiritual body and make them new, tender, and responsive! He can take out what is hard, stony, stubborn, rebellious, hurt, angry, embittered, depressed, filled with anxiety, or consumed by jealousy and make it all new again. What an amazing life we could lead if we would just allow the Lover of our soul to take control and make us new again! Can you imagine who or what you might become if you would just let go of the things of this world? Who would you be, what would you be able to accomplish if you were free from the carnal captivity all these worldly things, feelings that keep us imprisoned? What name is on the handcuffs you wear? Depression? Anxiety? Bitterness? Jealousy? Pain? Illness? Anger? Guilt? Addiction? What is it that holds you back from experiencing the full blessing God has for you? Ask God to reveal it to you, give it to Him, and be set free! Only you can do it. Those handcuffs can define you if you allow it, or you can seek the freedom that God offers and let His love, mercy, compassion, guidance, and freedom define who you are supposed to be. Aren't you tired of that prison cell? God has the key! Call out to God and be set free!

Thought #13

Deut. 4:24: "For the Lord your God is a consuming fire, a jealous God."

Make no mistake, God is not jealous of you. God is jealous for you. God is jealous concerning you because He wants to protect you from anything that would rob you of your uniqueness or threaten your relationship with Him. Put no god before Him and His commandments, and He will put nothing or no one before the desires of your heart. He will supply everything you need. He is jealous for you and your heart. Commit yourself to Him, and He will commit Himself to you.

Thought #14

Second Tim. 2:15–16: "Be diligent to present yourself approved to God, a worker who does not need to be ashamed, rightly dividing the word of truth. But shun profane and idle babblings, for they will increase to more ungodliness."

Have you ever found yourself in a conversation that deep in your spirit you know is wrong? Walk away! Walk away as fast as you can. Oh, I know you will hear a little whisper in your ear, "You can't just walk away. That would be rude!" or "Just wait until there is a break in the conversation and excuse yourself." Friend, I'm telling you now, if you wait for that, it's too late! Anything you hear or say cannot be unheard or unsaid. There's a reason the Bible says to shun that kind of situation. If your spirit man cringes even a little bit, it's time to walk away. Be sensitive to what your spirit tells you, and you won't have to justify anything to yourself, to others, or to God. There is no shame in walking away from an ungodly situation! If you don't hear it, you can't dwell on it or spread it. Just walk away! Don't include your ears, eyes, words, or thoughts in conversations that God would not approve of.

Thought #15

Luke 5:13: "Lord, if You are willing…"

Father, I don't know how you will do it, I don't know when you will do it, but I'm going to believe You anyway! Have you ever prayed for something only God can do? Have you prayed for it with your whole heart, mind, and strength? Jesus said, "Ask in My name, believing, and it will be yours." It must also be in His will and His timing. He will not give you something that will, at some point, be detrimental to you. He will not give you something before you are ready or fit for it. The secret to answered prayers is total submission to God and His will.

Lord, if You are willing, I will wait with hope and confidence. In Jesus' name, I pray, trust, and believe. Amen.

Thought #16

Second Cor. 5:7: "For we walk by faith, not by sight."

We love by faith, trusting that person will love us back. But sometimes they don't. We sleep by faith, trusting we will wake up in the morning. But sometimes we don't. We breathe by faith, trusting that next breath. But sometimes that next breath doesn't come. So why do we have trouble trusting the one person who cannot lie, who promises to never leave us, never forsake us, always provide for us, and always protect us? If we can close our eyes at night trusting that they will open in the morning, then why can't we trust God for everything else? For it is God who provides you that next breath, that next morning, and that person who will love you forever. You can trust Him with everything you have! You can trust Him with your life, your spouse, your children, your finances, your job, and your ministry. Everything you give Him, He will take and make it better! Trust Him! Walk by faith in all you do and watch what He does!

Thought #17

Gal. 5:25: "Since we are living by the Spirit, let us follow the Spirit's leading in every part of our lives."

This doesn't mean you need to ask God what color shirt you need to put on in the morning. But if you are a child of God and you sense He is speaking to you about something, do not jump to conclusions or jump ahead and charge in full force. Make sure you have clear guidance on what He is saying and where He wants you to go with it. Let Him work in you so He can work through you. Pay attention to the go, stop, and yield signs in your life.

Thought #18

Rom. 12:9: "Don't just pretend to love others. Really love them. Hate what is wrong. Hold tightly to what is good."

So many times, we just give lip service to this verse. Of course we love them! Well, we say we love others, but do we? We are commanded to love everyone, really love them, but do we? Really? What about that person who talked bad about you? What about that person who stabbed you in the back? What about that person that lied to you or about you? What about that person that took what was yours? What about that person that just rubs you the wrong way, the one that cut you off in traffic, the one that does nothing at work but takes all the credit? Or the one that spoke to you while you were in a bad mood? The one that offended you by something they inadvertently said or did? Paul said, "Hate what is wrong and hold tight to what is good." Hate the sin, but love the person. If we cannot separate the sin from the person, then we too have sinned and offended God. Hold tight to what is good, which is your salvation and your relationship with God. If you hold on to God, which is good, his Spirit will not let you hate that person, regardless of the offense they committed. Forgiveness is a hard thing! Jesus had to die to bring about our forgiveness; surely we can do no less. We do not have to die physically, but we do have to kill our fleshly desire for retribution. Hold tight to what is good and find peace instead of bitterness and sin. Without love and forgiveness in your heart, sin enters in. And you have left place for the enemy to take up residence. Don't just pretend to love others. Really love them! Hate what is wrong, but hold tightly to what is good. In other words, you can hate the sin, but you must love the sinner. Yes, for the most part they know what they are doing is wrong. But so did you and God still loved you, still died for you, and still pursues you. How can we do any less than what we are commanded to do? If we don't, then we are liars and hypocrites. Remember disobedience is sin and sin is evil.

Thought #19

1 John 4:4: "He who is in you is greater than he who is in the world."

There's nothing you can't do as long as Jesus lives inside you. There is nothing you can't overcome, there is nothing or no one that can block your path as long as you are walking that path with Jesus. There's no mountain so high you can't climb it, no valley so low you can't navigate it, no wave so big you can't ride it, no storm so loud you can't silence it, as long as you have Jesus living on the inside. Every new day will bring a new adventure or a new disaster; how you come through it depends on Who you let handle it. The One who longs to live inside you can turn that disaster into blessings. If you haven't already invited Jesus into your heart, then I encourage you to have an intimate conversation with Him right now. Invite Him in and hang on to every promise He ever made and watch what happens! If He already lives inside you, then go to His Word and trust Who and what you find there.

Thought # 20

Isa. 26:3–4: "You will keep perfect peace all who trust in You! Trust in the Lord always, for the Lord God is the eternal Rock."

Perfect peace! Can you even imagine it? Perfect peace, it's there for the taking. All we have to do is trust Someone who loves us with His whole heart, mind, and strength. Trust the One who cannot lie. Perfect peace will be found in perfect love. Keep your thoughts on God, keep your spiritual eyes and ears open, your heart supple, and He will bring you perfect peace. There is no situation so dire God cannot cover it with His love, mercy, grace, compassion, protection, and guidance. His blood covers everything—everything you are willing to trust Him with, that is. Perfect peace is found in the blood Jesus shed for you. He is waiting to share that perfect peace with you. Trust Him.

Thought #21

First Pet. 4:10: "As each one has received a gift, minister it to one another, as good stewards of the manifold grace of God."

God has given each of us a specific and special ability, or maybe more than one. These are our gift from Him. Everyone gets this gift. Everyone! Yes, that means you! However, this gift is not for you! This isn't even a gift we can claim ownership of. God plants it in us so that He can use it to help others. We are only the vessel! And before you say, "God has not planted, gifted, or birthed anything in me," ask yourself these questions. What am I good at? What do I love to do? What might be hidden deep inside me, that has yet to surface? I, myself, love to see people smile. I love to see a frown or tear turn into a smile! I love to watch joy replace sorrow. This makes me an encourager! I also love to pray for people, some would call that a prayer warrior. You may say, "Well that's not much, I thought you were talking about the gifts as in 1 Cor. 12." To that I say, "I encourage you to read 1 Cor. 12:4-6." If God uses a person to speak kind, uplifting words to someone with a broken heart and those words encourage this brokenhearted person, is that not healing? If you are having a conversation with someone and God uses you to help them understand something better, is that not imparting knowledge or even wisdom? These are only a few examples. First Cor. 12:4-6 says (paraphrased and shortened) there are different kinds of gifts, different kinds of service, and different kinds of working, but in all of them and in everyone, it is the same God at work. So before you say you don't have a gift, I encourage you to ask God to reveal that which He has planted in you and let Him help someone else.

Thought # 22

Ps. 40:1–2: "I waited patiently for the Lord to help me, and He turned to me and heard my cry. He lifted me out of the pit of despair, out of the mud and the mire. He set my feet on solid ground and steadied me as I walked along."

There's no place too far or so deep that the Lord can't hear you and come to where you are. There is no pit so full of sorrow, pain, anger, bitterness, depression, or anxiety that He can't pull you out. There's no sin so black that He can't wash it white as snow. Call out to Him! He will hear and rescue you! If you are lost, all it takes is a contrite, repentant heart. If you are saved and have become distracted by the enemy, the world, or maybe life just got in the way, call out! Regardless of where you are or what you've done, He will hear you. He is waiting and listening intently. He knows your voice. He will come when you call. Trust Him for all you need. He is faithful to His promises and to His children. He will come!

Thought # 23

Joel 2:25: "I will repay you for the years the locusts have eaten."

The locusts were one of the plagues God sent down on Egypt that ate everything in sight. And in years past, they were a very real enemy to the farmer. What has the enemy taken from you? Your peace, or maybe your joy? In what area has the "locust" eaten? Family? Home? Finances? Heart? Body? Spirit? This is your chance to take back what the enemy has taken from you. This is God's promise to repay all that you've lost. What are you waiting on? Think about how He repaid Job; Job was repaid much more than he lost. God never does anything in small measures! Give to God what is God's, stand on His promises, and let Him give to you everything your enemy took. If you would just trust Him, you would find that He will bless you with more than you lost. The more you learn to depend on Him, the more you are blessed. What have you got to lose?

Thought #24

John 12:26: "Anyone who wants to serve Me must follow Me, because my servants must be where I am. And the Father will honor anyone who serves Me."

It has been said, "Don't let your past mistakes keep you from your future possibilities." God has a plan, but to find out what it is you *must* follow Him to where He leads. He is *not* behind you in the past. If you allow Him, He will be in your present and in your future. He will guide you to heights your imagination could never take you! If you would just trust Him. Lk. 18:27 says, "God can do what men cannot." He can move mountains, He can calm seas, He can restore life where there was none, and He can heal the broken. What is it that you need? It can be yours, if you choose to follow the Lord. Become His child, honor Him, follow Him, and He will take care of you, your circumstance, your struggle, your storm, your health, your finances, your family, your fears. There is *nothing* God can't do! Follow Him, honor Him, serve Him, praise and worship Him, and He will honor you and bless you beyond your wildest dreams!

Thought #25

John 3:30: "He must increase, but I must decrease."

What's got you worried? Situations? Circumstances? Ministry? Take yourself out of the equation and watch what God will do! He is all-powerful. He is all-knowing. He has seen the beginning from the end, because He is already there. He already knows what you need; get out of His way and let Him have His way in whatever it is that has you worried!

Thought #26

Luke 1:37 "For with God nothing will be impossible."

That's it! That's all it says! There is no "if," no "or," no "except for"! *Nothing!* Nothing you can say, nothing you can do, nothing you will ever need will be impossible for God. Nothing! Need mercy? He's got it! Need grace? He has that in abundance. Need compassion, healing, love, comfort, peace, joy, concern, freedom, strength, boldness, courage, deliverance? He's got you covered! You say, "Nah, I got that. I need a job, husband, wife vehicle, home, etc." Guess what? He's got those too! There's *nothing* impossible for God. Did you get that? *Nothing*! There's no need so big He can't fill it. There's no sin so black He can't wash it, cover it, and erase it. All you have to do is be His child, walk an upright life before Him. Get aligned with God, His Word, and His will, and watch what happens! Everything you truly need will be waiting for you.

Thought # 27

Matt. 5:4: God blesses those who mourn, for they will be comforted.

I love the way this verse does not specify what is being mourned! Some mourn for a life they no longer have, some mourn for a life they never had, some mourn for loved ones that have yet to come to Christ, and we all have lost people that we mourn deeply for. This verse doesn't specify what is being mourned for, but it does say that we will be comforted! Mourning people or things is a heavy burden to carry. Why don't you let God lighten your burden? I pray you will give it to Him and let Him comfort you as He has promised to do. His comfort is beyond anything you will ever experience.

Thought # 28

Luke 11:9–10: "So I say to you, ask, and it will be given to you; seek, and you will find; knock and it will be opened to you. For everyone who asks, receives, and he who seeks finds, and to him who knocks it will be opened."

If you are His child, He will give you what you need. It might not be the exact thing you asked for, but it will be the best thing for you. God gives only His very best to those who love and obey Him. What do you need? How badly do you need it? What's it worth to you? What are you willing to do or to give up for it? How important is it to you? Are you willing to submit your will to obtain God's will, thereby having all that God wants to give you? There is so much more that God wants to give you! What you ask for is just the tip of the iceberg! No matter how big your request may be, God will trump it with what He wants to give you. Child of God, when you pray, voice your needs, your wants, and your concerns and ask God to take care of them. Be brave. Add not my will, but Yours. He is waiting to give you *His* very best, so do not limit Him with what you think you need. Let Him give you what you truly need.

Thought #29

Luke 11:1: "Lord, teach us to pray."

Father, I ask that You teach us to pray. Teach us to pray in a manner that is not amiss. Teach us to pray in a way that will shake the gates of heaven. Teach us to pray in a way that even the gates of hell tremble. Teach us to pray for others as fervently as we pray for ourselves. Teach us to pray for our enemies as though they were our children. Teach us to pray unselfishly for our lost loved ones. Teach us to pray with love in our hearts. Teach us to pray with Your heart for family, friends, enemies, and strangers. Teach us to pray persistently and not lose heart while waiting for those prayers to be answered. Lord, teach us to pray Your will, not ours, and mean it. In Jesus' name, I pray, trust, and believe. Amen.

Thought #30

Isa. 61:3: "To appoint unto them that mourn in Zion, to give unto them beauty for ashes, the oil of joy for mourning, the garment of praise for the spirit of heaviness; that they might be called trees of righteousness, the planting of the Lord, that He might be glorified."

Beauty for ashes, oil of joy, a garment of praise! What a beautiful picture this promise paints! Many of us suffer from depression caused by loneliness, grief, illness, regrets, worry about bills, fear or worry about children, parents, or siblings. There are so many things the enemy will use against us to put us in bondage. But this verse gives us a promise of beauty, joy, praise, and deliverance from everything that would steal these things from us. When you feel that spirit of darkness begin to descend, before it has a chance to take hold and drag you down into that familiar pit, *stop* what you are doing, get up, go turn your praise music on, turn it up, and start to *sing*! Sing until you have victory! That darkness will flee! The enemy will depart as the praise will lift that garment of heaviness! If the very name of Jesus can put the enemy on the run, what can the praises sang in His name do? Praise gives you *courage*! Praise gives you *boldness*! Praise gives you *peace*! Praise gives you *power* from on high! Use it and receive God's promise!

Thought #31

Prov. 15:3: "The Lord is watching everywhere, keeping His eye on both the evil and the good."

Be careful what you say, do, and think. God is always watching and listening. Even when you think no one sees, God always does. There are consequences to everything we do, good and bad! Be careful of your words, thoughts and actions! Think first, what consequence will this bring? Before you think that, say that, or do that, remember God is watching! Ask yourself, what will God think when He sees this?

Thought #32

John 14:1: "Don't let your hearts be troubled. Trust in God, and trust also in Me."

Worry and fear are *un*natural emotions. Think for just a moment, what are babies afraid of? What are small children afraid of? *Nothing*! Children believe they can do *anything*! God does not give us a spirit of fear, but of power! We are not born with fear, worry, hate, or bitterness. We are born with a spirit of power, wonder, and love. It is a spirit of mistrust that we develop as we grow older that enable these other spirits to move in. If we trusted our heavenly Father as a child trusts its earthly mother or father, then we too would live a life of power, wonder, and love! Everything we read in the Bible promises we can trust God to take care of us. Trust the promise! Trust the Word! Trust your heavenly Father as completely as you once trusted your earthly father/mother. We have nothing to lose and everything to gain! Come to Jesus as a little child, and He will renew that spirit of power! Trust the Lord, and He will take care of you!

Ps. 84:5: Blessed is the man whose strength is in You.

Thought #33

James 3:10–12: "Out of the same mouth proceed blessing and cursing… Does a spring send forth fresh water and bitter from the same opening?… Thus *no* spring yields both salt water and fresh."

We prove who we follow, who we obey, what we believe, and who we really are by the words that flow from our mouths. We cannot bless or praise (fresh water) and curse (bitter water) man with the same mouth. The Bible says what comes out of our mouth comes from our heart. No spring (heart) yields both salt and fresh. Therefore, we cannot bless/love God and curse/hate man. Fresh and bitter cannot come from the same opening!

Thought # 34

Ps. 34:1: "I will praise the Lord at all times. I will constantly speak His praises."

Don't forget to thank the Lord for everything He has done for you. I want to encourage you to stop and think for just a moment. Ask yourself, what has God done for me lately? First, you can start with He woke you up this morning. You had a bed to wake up in, there was a roof over your head, and you had food to eat. You have people that love you, and if you are very blessed, you have people that will pray for you. These are all tangible things that we can thank God for, but what about those mundane things we never even think about? What about the smile from a total stranger that put a smile on your face? Or that person that held the door open so you could walk through first? Or what about that parking spot closer to the grocery store door? Or better yet, that person who let you go first at the checkout counter? We all love that one. What about that baby who was barely able to sit alone in the grocery buggy that waved to you and, for some reason, brightened your day? Or the person who said, "I'm praying for you," without knowing your situation, or how badly you needed to hear it? Or that coworker that went out of their way to help you finish up something when they probably should have been working on their own stuff? Or the safe drive home you had from wherever you were? Did you remember to thank God for any of those moments? None of these things happen by accident or coincidence! They happen because God knows what you need and will fill every need. There are so many wonderful things that happen in our lives on a daily basis that provide opportunities to praise God. But most of the time, we let them slip by without a thought. Stay alert, keep your eyes open, and watch what God does for you today. Don't forget to thank Him for each one. I bet you will be very surprised by how many times in just one day you end up saying, "Thank you, Jesus!"

Thought #35

John 16:33: "I have told you all this so that you may have peace in Me. Here on earth you will have many trials and sorrows. But take heart, because I have overcome the world."

Take heart! There is nothing new in the heavens, on the earth, below the earth, or in your life that God cannot handle. His power is absolute! He has every answer you will ever need. It does not matter how dark your valley is, how loud, scary, or big your storm is, or how bad the enemy bares his teeth at you! God has already overcome it and declared victory over it! He offers His strength, His courage, His peace, His love, and His protection. All you have to do is ask for and accept it. He is waiting for you to take the first step; He will do the rest!

Thought #36

Ps. 28:6–7: "May honor and thanks be given to the Lord, because He has heard my prayer. The Lord is my strength and my safe cover. My heart trusts in Him, and I am helped."

How often have I cried out to my Jesus? How often has He heard my cry? How often has he answered my prayer? How often have I found strength in my Lord? How often has He protected me? I'll tell you how often! *Every time*! There has never been a time that I cried "Lord" that He did not hear me! There has never been even one time that He did not answer my prayer. Every time I cried out, I found strength in Him, knowing He heard me and knowing the answer was already on the way. From the very moment I invited Him in, He was there loving me, protecting me, and perfecting me. Does my flesh sometimes doubt? Yes! But my heart trusts in Him and I ask forgiveness for my foolishness, and He helps me. I give Him honor, thanks, and glory, for without Him I am nothing. I encourage you to invite Him in and let Him take care of you. Cry out! He will hear you! He will give strength and be your safe cover. There is nothing He won't do for you! Test Him and see! His love is true and faithful!

Thought # 37

John 11:40: Jesus said to her, "Did I not say to you that if you would believe you would see the glory of God?"

I have seen chains of addiction broken! I have seen gangland ties crumble! I have seen families reunited! I have seen demons flee at the sound of His name! I have been saved from sin, death, and divorce! I have been healed! I have been set free from pain, hurt, anger, guilt, shame, and bitterness. I have watched as my prayers and the prayers of others have been answered. All this came not because of anything I did, but because I believe! I believed that a man willingly gave His life for me! I believe He loved me and that His power and glory are unlimited! There is nothing He cannot do for you, if you would just believe! What is it that you need? Believe, and you *will* see the glory of God! Believe!

Thought #38

Gal. 4:19: "Until Christ is formed in you."

This is where God's vision for your life starts! Until Christ is formed in you, you will not have the blessings, or all that God's vision entails for you. You have no idea what great and wonderful things God has planned for you! You think your life is good now? This is nothing compared to what God wants for you and will give you. What in the world have you got to lose by accepting the abundance God wants to pour into your life? Is what you have right now so wonderful it can't be improved upon? Let Christ be formed in you and watch what God does with what you have! Nothing you have at this moment is as great as the blessings that are waiting to be poured out into your life straight from the hands of God! So really, what do you have to lose?

Thought #39

Col. 3:12–13: "Since God chose you to be the holy people He loves, you *must* clothe yourselves with tenderhearted mercy, kindness, humility, gentleness, and patience. Make allowance for each other's faults, and forgive anyone who offends you, Remember, the Lord forgave you, so you *must* forgive others."

Must forgive—seems to me that leaves us no other option and no room for justification. Especially since the Bible also tells us (paraphrased) if we want the Lord's forgiveness, we *must* forgive others. He chose us because He loves us. He chose *you* because He has a plan specifically for you. He chose us to be His holy people. We cannot be holy with a heart filled with hate, anger, bitterness, jealousy, or the need for vengeance. Only those without sin are allowed to throw rocks! We all have sinned; that is why we *must* make allowance for others' faults. Besides, it's not our place to judge! His commandment is to love, not judge, for surely we will be judged with the same measure. What a scary thought! Clothe yourself with tenderhearted mercy, kindness, humility, gentleness, patience, and pray that God will teach you to love others the way He loves them, even those who've lied to or about you, left you, stabbed you in the back, or taken what was yours. Consider what Jesus offered up for your forgiveness! Don't let what He accomplished be done in vain. Ask Him to help you forgive that person.

Thought #40

Phil. 4:13: "For I can do everything through Christ, who gives me strength."

There is nothing you'll ever have to face alone as long as you have Jesus in your life. God will carry you through every trial, every sorrow, every mess, and every temptation you will ever face. He will be your strength and the courage you need to get through it. Through Him you will have healing, peace, and joy.

Thought #41

Ps. 103:8: "The Lord is compassionate and merciful, slow to get angry and filled with unfailing love."

This is our example how we must be toward each other! How sad it must make the Lord for us to act toward each other with hate, anger, bitterness, rage, jealously, revenge, and malicious intent after all He has done for us! All He asks is that we love one another. He does not command that we love one another's faults or sins, but that we love each other as He loves us. How can we judge another's sin when we have so many of our own? Oh, we can try to justify our own sin saying, "At least my sin isn't that big!" But you know what? Sin is sin! Nowhere in the Bible does it mention that God has a rating system. If we are not doing what God's word instructs us to do, then we are in direct disobedience to God. We have sinned against God! Where would that be on man's rating scale? It doesn't matter to God how big or how little we think our sin might be. To Him, it's all the same. Love one another as your Father has loved you and let Him handle sin. That's His job anyway!

Thought #42

Prov. 20:9: "Who can say, 'I have cleansed my heart; I am pure and free from sin.'"

Lord, I ask You to reveal the sin still left in my life, my heart, my words, my thoughts, and my actions. Holy Ghost, have Your way with me. I cannot know all sin without Your sweet conviction poured out on me. I need You. I trust You to show me what must be changed, removed, and destroyed. In Jesus' name, I invite You in right now to cleanse my heart. Make me pure and free. In Jesus name, I pray, trust, and believe. Amen.

Thought #43

James 1:5–6: "If any of you lack wisdom, let him ask of God, that giveth to all men liberally, and upbraideth [doubt] not; and it shall be given to him. But let him ask in faith, nothing wavering. For he that wavereth is like a wave of the sea driven with wind and tossed."

Ask God for wisdom, and He will give it to you! It will guide you and keep you from making rash decisions that will take you down paths that lead away from God. Have you ever watched something being tossed around by a wave at the beach? It doesn't take long before whatever it is looks bruised, beat up, and eventually broken.

This is what happens to us without godly wisdom. We allow life, the world, and the enemy to toss us around with waves of anger, bitterness, hurt, illness, anxiety, depression, self-pity, jealousy, and eventually, hate for other and for ourselves. Ask God for wisdom, discernment, strength, courage, boldness, mercy, and compassion. He will give you all this and more! He will give you *everything* you need! All you have to do is ask believing and it *shall* be yours.

Thought #44

Prov. 1:4–5: "These proverbs will give insight to the simple, knowledge and discernment to the young. Let the wise *listen* to these proverbs and become even wiser. Let the man with understanding *receive* guidance."

Listen and receive…, insight, knowledge, discernment, understanding, and guidance! These are a Christian's true needs. As long as we love God and seek to obey His commandments, everything else will fall into place. Do not fear; God has promised to supply all your needs. All you need do is do what you know to do and let God handle the rest. Trust Him, listen to Him, and obey. He will not let you fail.

Thought #45

James 4:3: "Ye ask and receive not, because ye ask amiss, that ye may consume it upon your lusts."

What are you praying for? And more important, *why* are you praying for it? Is it because you *need* it, truly need it? Is the "need" being met? Has the prayer been answered? God promises to meet our every need, and God cannot lie. So if what you are praying for has yet to be answered, it may be a good idea to ask, "*Why* am I praying this prayer?" Sometimes, we ask for things that are good things, that are needed, but we ask for the wrong reasons, or possibly with selfish motives. If a prayer isn't being answered, or the answer seems to be taking a long time in coming, we should ask ourselves why. Is this a selfless prayer, or am I asking selfishly? We have to be honest with our answer; we are geared to justify to get what we want. Look deep, ask honestly, "Do I ask this for my flesh? Pride? Pleasure? Out of jealousy?" Do not be deceived; we all pray selfishly at times. If this prayer is truly important to you and has not been answered, then ask why. Maybe you aren't ready for the answer, maybe God has a reason to tarry, or maybe you have asked amiss! Only God knows the true answer, but He will reveal it to you if you ask Him. Be brave, be bold, be honest with God and with yourself, and watch what happens.

Thought #46

Jer. 29:11: "For I know the plans I have for you, says the Lord. They are plans for good and not for disaster, to give you a future and a hope."

Don't let the choices you make bring you disaster. Trust God's plan for your future. Become His child. Do what you know to do and trust God to handle the rest. His way is better than yours. Trust Him and His vision for your life.

Thought #47

First Pet. 1:15: "But as He who called you is Holy, you also be holy in all your conduct, because it is written, Be holy, for I am holy."

All your conduct! That means what you say, what you think, what you do! If what comes out of your mouth or your heart is ungodly, then you are disobeying God's order. We are commanded to be holy as He is holy. So if we are cussing, tearing another person down (regardless of what that person has said or done), being self-seeking, or causing strife of any kind, we are not serving the God of heaven. We are not obeying the command to be holy as He is holy. We all follow something or someone, and our thoughts, actions, and words prove just who we follow. Jam. 4:11 says, "Do not speak evil of one another." Be careful of what you say, think, and do for not only is the world watching and judging your actions, so is the God we claim to love, follow, and serve. Actions speak louder than words, so let not your actions speak against or grieve God.

James 5:9: "Do not grumble against one another, brethren, lest you be condemned. Behold, the Judge is standing at the door!"

Thought #48

Prov. 27:2: "Let someone else praise you, not your own mouth—a stranger, not your own lips."

People, strangers, extended family, more importantly your spouse and your children are watching you. What do they see? Is what they see praiseworthy? Would your children be proud to call you mother/father? Can the world say, "Yes, she belongs to Christ"? Can people look at you and your life and say, "I want what he has"? What do people see when they look at you? Can Christ look at you and say, with pride, "Yes, that one is mine"? People know you by the way you live, not just by what comes out of your mouth. What do they see? Is it praiseworthy?

Thought #49

John 15:12: "Love one another as I have loved you."

God loves us unconditionally, without reservation, without thought to what we did or might do. There is nothing we can do or could ever do that would make God not love us. And this is what He commands us to do to each other! The opposite of love is not hate; it is selfishness (Billy Graham). Could it be that we cannot love as God commands because we are too full of self? Maybe it's because we want what we want is or has become more important than what God wants. The main cause for disobedience (sin) is selfishness. God also commands that we love others as we love ourselves, but do we? We say we do, but do we? Again, our actions speak louder than our words!

(***Disclaimer*** God's love alone will not get you into heaven! The decision you make at His drawing is what gets you there! There is only one way to heaven!)

Thought #50

Ps. 91:4: "He will cover you with His feathers. He will shelter you with His wings. His faithful promises are your armor and protection."

You know how everyone says, "God will not give you more than you can handle"? Well, I have always felt that was as far from the truth as you can get! If we can handle it all, then what's the point of having God in our life? I can give testimony to the many times the *only* way I made it through some things was because God and *only* God got me through it. There were a few times He had to pick me up and carry me through it or I would have never made it. There were also a couple times He had to drag me through it kicking and screaming! So yes, you will go through things you will not be able to handle on your own. *But* you do not have to handle it on your own. God will carry you through! I promise, if you have God in your life, He will carry you through it. Trust God to carry you to heights you've never before imagined!

Thought #51

James 5:16: "The earnest prayer of a righteous person has great power and produces wonderful results."

First Cor. 15:57: "God gives us the victory through our Lord Jesus Christ."

You know that thing in your life that keeps making your life miserable? That thing that no matter what you do or say, it keeps defeating you? Read these two verses and let God speak to you and reveal to you how to defeat that thing. God can destroy the mess in your life and turn it into a life of joy and peace. But you have to talk to Him! Not a two-second, distracted prayer. Take a few minutes and get away from everything and everyone and *talk* to Him without any interference. Pray with determination to reach His ears and His heart. He will hear you!

Thought #52

Matt. 11:28: "Come to Me, all you who labor and are heavy laden, and I will give you rest."

Jesus knows what you are going through! He sees the burden you are carrying. He cares for you and your burdens enough to have died for you. Don't you think He cares enough to carry your burden for you? He carried the cross because of us. Why would He not carry this burden as well? You can bet it isn't as heavy as the cross was! Won't you accept His offer? Come to Me, and I will give you rest. Aren't you tired of carrying that weight around? What have you got to lose by laying it at His feet? Give Him a chance! Trust Him! Let Him carry your burden and lighten your load. He will set you free, if you would just allow it!

Thought #53

Rom. 12:17: "Never pay back evil with more evil. Do things in such a way that everyone can see you are honorable."

People believe what they see more that what they hear, so live your life in a way that everyone sees you are an honorable person. Jealous people will always talk behind your back. Mean spirited, hate-filled people will always want you as miserable as they are. But you do not have to sink to their level. Be better than they are, do not repay evil with evil. Be judged by the honorable life you live, not by hate, jealousy, and bitterness spewing from your heart. The Bible quotes God as saying, "I will take revenge; I will pay them back," so do what you know to do and let God handle the ungodly. It is His job, and He has had eternity to perfect it. Live an honorable, godly life, and that's what you will be judged by, by the world and by God. Job lived an honorable life, and look what God did for him. Everything that was taken from Job, God gave back double! Not only that, but God handled Job's enemies. Live an honorable life and be blessed as Job was blessed.

James 5:11: "As you know, we count as blessed those who have persevered. You have heard of Job's perseverance and have seen what the Lord finally brought about. The Lord is full of compassion and mercy."

Thought #54

Phil. 1:6: "And I am certain that God, who began the good work within you, will continue His work until it is finally finished."

If you do not let the Lord finish what He started, you will never have what you want or what you need. You will never be completely happy. It's up to you; we can either obey God or keep doing what we want to do. Best advice ever: let God finish what He started.

Thought #55

Eph. 4:2: "Always be humble and gentle. Be patient with each other, making allowance for each other's faults because of your love."

You notice this verse does not say, "Make allowance for each other's faults because they deserve it." It says, "Because of your love." Verse after verse commands us to be humble and gentle. Even more verses command us to be loving and forgiving. In fact, the Bible states in Mt. 6:14 that if we want forgiveness, then we must forgive. Even if that person has cut you to your heart, even if that person never asks forgiveness, you must forgive, or you will not be forgiven. So regardless of whether they deserve it or not, we must forgive them! Forgiving or making allowances does not make them or what they did right, but it will certainly make you right. It won't be easy, and you most certainly will not be able to do it within yourself. But God will help you if you ask. The Bible says ask believing and it shall be yours. With God's help, you can do this, you must do this! Without this, you will not be forgiven. This isn't just my opinion; this is God's command. Trust God. He will bring you through this and make you a better person from it.

Thought #56

Ps. 71:5: "For You have been my hope, O Sovereign Lord, my confidence since my youth."

Lord, You are my hope, my confidence, my strength, my joy, my peace, and my comfort. You are my rock, my provider, and my protector. Nothing can touch me that You do not allow. I am covered by Your blood; therefore, the enemy cannot touch me without touching You first. Those that come against me must come through You to get to me. What a privilege it is to be Your child! Thank you, Father, for being everything I need. In Jesus' name I pray, trust, and believe. Amen.

Thought #57

Mark 11:14: "Whatever things you ask when you pray, believe that you receive them, and you will have them."

First John 3:22: "And whatever we ask, we receive from Him, because we keep His commandments and do the things that pleasing in His sight."

Three things must happen before God will hear and answer our prayers.

First, you must truly belong to Him. If you are not His child, He is not obligated to hear or answer your prayer. That is not saying that He doesn't love you. He loves you with His whole heart! But just that love does not get us into heaven, nor does it obligate God to hear and answer our prayers.

Second, we must obey His Word. Not just the Ten Commandments we learn as children, but His whole word! If we want to receive the promises in His Word, then we must be willing to follow His instructions as well. We cannot have one without the other.

Third, our thoughts, actions, and words must be pleasing to Him. We cannot think, talk, act, or live like hell and expect the blessings of heaven to pour out on us. Love God with all your strength. Obey God and live to please Him with all your might and determination. Ask and ye shall receive! It's not as hard as you think.

Thought #58

Prov. 19:21: "You can make many plan, but the Lord's purpose will prevail."

It doesn't matter what we plan to do, how we plan to live our lives, what we think we want. The will of God will be done in our lives. We can either submit to God's will or we can spend our lives battling Him. What's the point of constantly struggling with circumstances, people, job, and finances when all we have to do is submit to God's will and all those struggles will fix themselves? No, I'm not saying life will be perfect, but at least you won't be struggling to get ahead, keep your head above water, with anger, bitterness, jealousy, hurt, depressed, or anxiety ridden. You will have peace and joy in your life! The struggles you do encounter won't be the huge battles you're fighting right now. What have you got to lose? Trust the Lord to handle your battle, and victory will be yours! Submit to God's purpose and plans and use the time you spend struggling for something more worthwhile!

Thought #59

Prov. 15:1: "A gentle answer deflects anger, but harsh words make tempers flare."

Stand your ground, but keep your words sweet and gentle. Even the devil cannot effectively argue with a gentle spirit. Gentle does not mean wimpy, so stand your ground and don't let the enemy have what you've worked so hard for. Use gentle words when dealing with an argumentative spirit. Anything else will cause tempers to flare even higher, and words that cannot be taken back will slip out. Gentleness wins out every time. Jesus was as gentle as a lamb, but He was also as strong as a lion. He is our example! Imitate Him in all you do.

Thought #60

Deut. 31:6: "So be strong and courageous! Do not be afraid and do not panic before them. For the Lord your God will personally go ahead of you. He will neither fail you nor abandon you."

There's nothing or no one you have to be afraid of! There's no mountain too high, no sea to wide, no human too fierce, no enemy so ferocious that God has not already overcome! Whatever is ahead of you, know that God has already been there! He has spoken peace to you and your situation. Trust Him, He will guide you through it and bring you out the other side a stronger, better, wiser person. Don't be afraid; if you belong to God, then just like everything else you've been through, He's got you on this one too! If you do not belong to Him, the remedy is simple! Become His child! He will take care of you! He will not fail you, He will not abandon you! Trust Him! He is worthy!

Thought #61

Ps. 103:1–3: "Let all that I am praise the Lord; with my whole heart, I will praise His holy name/Let all that I am praise the Lord; may I never forget the good things He does for me. He forgives all my sins and heals all my diseases."

Never forget! Look at all He has given you! Have you thanked Him for it? Regardless of what we think or believe, without God, we'd not have any of this. Have you thanked Him lately? Or do we, without even thinking about it, take Him, His love, kindness, compassion, faithfulness, mercy, and grace for granted? What He gave you was His to give. He gave it because He loves you! But just like with Job, He could allow it to *all* be taken away in an instant! Praise Him for what He has done!

He is my God, and I will put no other God before Him. Without Him, I would be nothing! Without Him, I would have nothing! He is all I need, because with Him I have everything!

Thought #62

Isa. 40:31: "But those who trust in the Lord will find new strength. They will soar high on wings like eagles. They will run and not grow weary, they will walk and not faint."

It doesn't matter what you're going through. It doesn't matter that there doesn't seem to be a light at the end of your tunnel. It doesn't matter if the waves are crashing over your head or that the undertow seems to be pulling you farther and farther away from shore into deeper waters! If you have the Lord, it doesn't matter what your limited human brain, eyes, or emotion screams at you! It doesn't matter, because God isn't seeing it through *your* perspective! God has already seen through the tunnel, calmed the waves, and spoken the undertow into submission. Let your spirit see it from God's perspective, and all your fears will subside! He will give you the strength to walk through the fire without fainting, run the race without growing weary, and soar to heights unimaginable! Trust Him; He has already read the last page of your book, and by His hand, you have won every battle, beaten every enemy, and collected all the spoils of war! Read your story from God's perspective, and you will see victory on every page!

Thought #63

Heb. 10:22: "Let us go right into the presence of God with sincere hearts fully trusting Him. For our guilty consciences have been sprinkled with Christ's blood to make us clean, and our bodies have been washed with pure water."

If you have been washed in God's blood, all past mistakes have been washed clean. Don't go back and relive those mistakes. They are so much more costly the second time around. Regardless of what the day brings, you can trust God to get you through it. But only if you give it to Him. Ask Him to join you in the battle and be assured of total victory, instead making Him sit on the sideline watching you struggle and lose. Trust Him! He will get you through it!

Thought #64

Gal. 6:7–8: "Don't be misled—you cannot mock the justice of God. You will always harvest what you plant. Those who live only to satisfy their own sinful nature will harvest decay and death from that sinful nature. But those who live to please the Spirit will harvest everlasting life from the Spirit."

Sinful nature is *anything* you say, think, or do that *does not* line up with who God is, what He stands for, and what He commands us to say, think, and do. The Bible says what you say, do, and think comes from what is in your heart. Watch your mouth (unruly tongue), your actions, and your thoughts lest they cause you to sin and bring shame and dishonor to God's name. Do not be misled; if you call yourself a child of God, the world and the enemy are watching and waiting for you to prove otherwise. Who we are, how we act, and what comes out of our mouth speaks truth as to who we belong to.

Thought #65

Phil. 4:6: "Don't worry about anything; instead pray about everything. Tell God what you need, and thank Him for all He has done."

Thank you, Jesus, for caring about what worries me and the reassurance that You know my heart, You understand my concerns, and You have everything under control. I know that there is nothing beyond Your control. Thank you for handling those things I cannot. Thank you for speaking peace into every situation. Thank you for

Your love, mercy, grace, compassion, power, concern, and attentiveness. Without You, where would I be? Thank you, Father, for taking care of me! In Jesus' name, I pray, trust, and believe that whatever I face, I face it with You and will have victory over it all. I am Yours and I am not alone! In Jesus' name, I pray. Amen.

Thought #66

First John 4:4: "But you belong to God, my dear children. You have already won a victory over those people, because the Spirit who lives in you is greater than the spirit who lives in the world."

If you have given your life to God at any time in your life, live like it! There is no person, no thing, no situation, no struggle, no trial, no storm that can defeat you. You are wonderfully made in the image of the one true God, and if He resides in your heart, then His victory resides there also. Believe in and trust the One who gave you life. Trust that He will take care of you, protect you, and provide for you. There is joy, peace, and comfort in knowing that He loves and fights for you. There is nothing God your Father will not do for you! If He is not your Father, none of His promises belong to you. This is not my opinion. Read your Bible; it will tell you the same. He loves you as much as He loves one of His children, but His promises, blessings, presence, protection, and provision are reserved for His blood-bought children. Invite Him to become your God, Father, Lord, Master, Friend, Defender, Provider. He is just waiting for one word from you, and He will happily become all this and more!

Thought #67

Prov. 1:8: "Hear the instruction of your Father."

Listen to what God has been telling you. Time is running out. Pay attention, do what you know He wants you to do. Your spirit has heard and will obey if you will allow it. You have been called; answer it before it is too late. You say you don't know what God has called you to do; let me enlighten you. You have been called to do exactly what we've all been called to do. You have been called to join God's children. You have been called to live for Him. You have been called to serve Him. But most importantly, you have been called to be loved by Him as His most prized possession. Come to where He is and receive your blessing, your healing, your calling, your gift. *It* and He is waiting with open arms.

Thought #68

Gal. 5:25: "Since we are living by the Spirit, let us follow the Spirit's leading in every part of our lives."

Listen to what the Spirit of God is telling you. You know what the Holy Ghost is prompting you to do. You feel it in your heart and your spirit longs to obey. The Bible says, "Do not quench the Spirit." By quenching the Spirit, we sin. Listen and obey before it's too late. Nowhere in the Bible does it say, it will happen when you are ready. It's not about *your* will. Think about it: where has *your* will gotten you? It's about God's will, God's way, God's plan, God's purpose, and God's vision. We are to love, live, and obey God's Word—all of it. Follow His lead, listen to the prompting of His Spirit. Stop rebelling. It's not about what you want; it's about what you need! Listen and obey, listen and be blessed, listen and have a new, better life!

Thought #69

Second Cor. 3:17: "For the Lord is the Spirit, and wherever the Spirit of the Lord is, there is Freedom."

Aren't you sick of the way things are? Aren't you tired of the same old same? Every day, day in and day out, same, same, same! No change! Aren't you sick of it? How long has it been since you felt real joy? Real peace? Real freedom from worry, fear, depression, anxiety, pain, bitterness, or anger? How long has it been since you felt financial freedom? Mental freedom? Emotional freedom? Spiritual freedom? Aren't you ready for a change? Are you ready for *freedom*? What will it take? What do you have to lose? *Get up! Take a chance!* Freedom is yours if you want it! Your heart, your mind, and your spirit are crying out, "*Freedom! Freedom! Freedom!*" What do you need to be free from? It's time to claim yours!

Thought #70

Ps. 119:45: "I will walk in freedom, for I have devoted myself to your commandments."

I walk in freedom because You have set me free. I will walk in freedom because Your Word has set me free to follow Your commandments. I walk in freedom from death, sin, pain, bitterness, hate, anger, and sorrow. I walk in freedom from the darkness of depression, anxiety, fear, and worry. I walk in freedom from jealousy and covetousness. I walk in freedom not because of who I am but because of who You are. I walk in freedom because I devote myself to live by Your Word and Your commandment to live free. I walk in freedom because I know truth. I walk in freedom because You said I could!

John 8:32: "And you will know the truth and the truth will set you free."

Thought #71

Matt. 7:1–3: "Judge not, that ye be not judge. For with what judgement ye judge, ye shall be judged: and with what measure ye mete, it shall be measured to you again. And why beholdest thou the mote that is in thy brother's eye, but considerest not the beam that is in thine own eye?"

We are called to love one another, not judge. We are called to bring joy to one another, not condemnation. We are called to encourage, edify, and lift up one another, not backbite and tear down. We are called to look to ourselves before looking to others. God has established a time and place for judging, and neither you nor I will be on the throne when it happens. God is on the throne, and we are not! And remember, if we take it upon ourselves to be the judge, we are risking being judged by the same measure by the ultimate judge. Whatever satisfaction we get from judging someone else is *not* worth it!

Thought #72

Ps. 66:16–20: "Come and listen, all you who fear God, and I will tell you what He did for me. For I cried out to Him for help praising Him as I spoke. If I had not confessed the sin in my heart, the Lord would not have listened. But God did listen! He paid attention to my prayer. Praise God, who did not ignore my prayer or withdraw His unfailing love for me."

Confess any sin in your heart to remove all that stands between you and God. He will hear you; He will answer you. He will fix whatever it is. Let God be your Father, your Friend, your Lord, your Rock, your Hiding Place, your Doctor, your Lawyer, your Strength, Peace, Comfort, and Joy. He will give you what you need, when you need it! Cry out to Him; He will hear and answer you. There is enormous power in prayer! All you have to do is confess, repent, and ask! Then start praising Him for what He will do.

Thought #73

Luke 6:46–47: "So why do you keep calling me "Lord, Lord!" when you don't do what I say? I will show you what it's like when someone comes to me, listens to my teaching, and then follows it."

Pay attention to what God is saying in this verse! Don't just call out to God when you are in trouble or need a prayer answered. Listen to what he says or shows you and then follow it. Spend a little time with Him every day, and you will learn to recognize His voice and His guidance. Don't be like those that think God is there to serve them and only seek Him when they need something. Talk to God, listen to God, read His Word, get to know Him, and do what He tells you to do. Or you can spend your life struggling in every situation. The choice is yours. Have a little talk with Jesus, tell Him what you need, thank Him for doing whatever He decides to do. Open your Bible and let God open your eyes!

Thought #74

Isa. 65:24: "I will answer them before they even call to Me. While they are still talking about their needs, I will go ahead and answer their prayers."

Ask me how real prayer is, how powerful prayer is! I know this because God healed me just last week from a headache so horrendous I could barely move. I made myself get out of bed, move to the recliner, and start praying. Mind you, this headache had been going on for nine days, getting worse every day. It was so bad my husband suggested I go to the hospital. But I knew God would heal me if I believed and was determined enough to do whatever it took to get healed. As I sat there praying, I literally felt God's hand rest on the back of my neck. It heated up the upper part of my back, my neck, and up inside my head to just above the left temple. I've *never* felt anything like it before, and within seconds, *all* my pain was gone! All of it! Without meds! Without anything but God's healing touch. I know it's real! Don't get me wrong; it didn't happen as soon as I prayed. In fact, I had been praying for nine days! But when I made myself get out of bed, I was determined I was going to pray until I shook the gates of heaven. I don't know if they shook or not, but I know I was heard and I know I was healed! I am still in awe of what the Lord did for me! This is not the first time I've been healed. But this is the first time I have actually felt God as it was happening. I have never felt the heat of God's healing hand laid upon me before.

Whatever you have need of, God is waiting to give it to you. Be persistent, be determined, have faith to believe God will do anything for you! He will give you everything you need if you just ask believing in Him, His power, His ability, His willingness, and His love for you. His grace, mercy, and compassion are yours for the asking. He is whatever you need! He has everything you need. Ask and it shall be yours.

Thought #75

Col. 1:10: "Then the way you live will always honor and please the Lord, and your lives will produce every kind of good fruit."

There is no better way for a Christian to honor and please the Lord than to live a life that proves you are who you say you are. If your lips and your life line up with God's Word, then you will produce every kind of good fruit and people will be won to Christ and the way you live will always honor and please the Lord. We cannot live like hell and expect to go to heaven. If you are truly a child of the one true living God, you will want to live in a manner that brings glory and honor to His name. Would you purposely bring shame and dishonor to your earthly parents? Of course not! Be careful, be diligent, and be determined! Live a life pleasing to your heavenly Father and watch what fruit He is able to produce through that life.

Thought #76

Luke 6:45: "A good person produces good things from the treasury of a good heart, and an evil person produces evil things from the treasury of an evil heart. What you say flows from what is in your heart."

Are we speaking death or life? Pain or comfort? Anger or peace? Bitterness, hate, and resentment? Or joy, encouragement, and love? What is in your heart? What is coming out of your mouth? Be careful of your words; they are the proof of the abundance of your heart. The Bible says the tongue holds the power of life and death. Which are you speaking? And whose life are you speaking it into? What are you speaking into your marriage, your children's lives, and your extended relationships? What are you speaking into your situations, your struggles, your storms, your very own life? Speak love! Speak encouragement! Speak kindness! Speak wisdom! Speak faith! Praise the Lord for what He is doing and what He is going to do! Produce good with your words. And remember what goes in will come out! Store up the fruit of the Spirit in your heart, and the fruit of the Spirit will flow from it.

Thought #77

Matt. 7:12: "In everything, do to others what you would have them do to you."

In everything! You cannot expect to be treated with goodness, gentleness, love, compassion, and respect unless that is the way you treat others. Will everyone treat you to the same love and respect you treat them with? Probably not everyone, but most will. But even more important than that is God will see your obedience and bless you for it. I know from experience that God's blessings go beyond anything you can imagine. Not only that, if you follow/obey Him with your whole heart, mind, and strength, He will handle those that persecute you. He can bring your enemies to kneel humbly at your feet. He has done it for me, and He will do it for you. Obey the Lord in everything, and He will pour out His blessings on you. Let Christ's gentleness and compassion flow through you and watch the change that takes place! Treat *everyone* the way you want them to treat you—yes, even that person that hurt you beyond words, especially that person. God has a plan for that person, and like it or not, you are a part of that plan. Don't only bless those that bless you; bless also those that, in your mind, deserve no blessing.

Thought #78

Prov. 15:1: "A gentle answer deflects anger, but harsh words make tempers flare."

Stand your ground, but keep your words sweet and gentle. Even the devil cannot effectively argue with a gentle spirit. Gentle does not mean wimpy, so stand your ground and don't let the enemy have what you've worked so hard for. Use gentle words when dealing with an argumentative spirit. Anything else will cause tempers to flare even higher, and words that cannot be taken back will slip out. Gentleness wins out every time. Jesus was as gentle as a lamb, but He was also as strong as a lion. He is our example! Imitate Him in all you do.

Thought #79

Prov. 23:7 "As he thinketh in his heart, so is he."

Think about that for a moment! Think about how much truth is in that short statement! As he thinketh in his heart, so he is. We become whatever is in our heart. If we have bitterness in our heart, then we live a bitter life. If we have a vengeful heart, then we live and waste our lives constantly looking for revenge. We live our lives controlled by what is in our heart. Pain, fear, worry, distrust, hate, anger, jealousy, etc. in our hearts control who we are, how we live, think, speak and act, and even who we spend our time with. Think about it for a moment! Is that truly how you want to spend the rest of your days? Do you really want these things to control who you are? Stop holding on to what has you enslaved! You can be free and completely delivered from the chains that bind you to that miserable life. You too can live a life full of joy, peace, love, and freedom! Ps. 25:1–2 "Lord, I give my life to You. I trust in You, my God"—this is all it takes! What on earth have you got to lose? Is what you have right now so wonderful you won't trade it for freedom to live a life full of joy, peace, and blessings beyond your wildest imagination? If it's not as wonderful as you thought it would be, if you aren't completely satisfied, you can always return to what you had before. My guess would be once you taste true freedom through Jesus Christ, you will *never* go back. Try it! What have you got to lose! He is waiting to break the chains that bind your heart. He is waiting to set you free!

Thought #80

Rom. 14:10–12: "So why do you condemn another believer? Why do you look down on another believer? Remember, we will all stand before the judgment seat of God. For the scriptures say, 'As surely as I live,' says the Lord, 'every knee will bend to me and every tongue will declare allegiance to God.' Yes, each of us will give a personal account to God."

Every person who has ever lived, is living now, and will ever live will come face to face with God to give an account of why they said and did all the things He has not already forgiven them for. Why did you say those things? Why did you do that? Why didn't you help that person carry his burden? Why didn't you love that person? Why did you treat them as if they were worthless? Why didn't you treat them the way you expect to be treated? Why did you think you were better? Who are you to judge another? Who are you to condemn? When every question has been answered, what will you hear: "Welcome home, dear child," or "Turn away. I know you not"? Think before you speak or act. God is watching, listening, and keeping record of all we say and do. We will all be judged for our own sins. Time for justification will be gone. Will we be found with blood on our hands? Will we be found blameless? Judging by the example of your life, what will your fate be?

Thought #81

First Pet. 3:1–2: "In the same way, you wives must accept the authority of your husbands. Then, even if some refuse to obey the Good News, your godly lives will speak to them without any words. They will be won over by observing your pure and reverent lives."

I can testify to this promise! Did it happen overnight? No! In fact, it took several years. God had to get *me* ready, to mature *me* enough to obey Him. I'm not saying there weren't moments of impatience, doubts, and even thoughts of giving up. But I never gave up. I prayed and prayed, and from the very beginning, the Lord spoke to my spirit and said, "Don't say a word, just keep living Me in front of him. It's not your job to save or change him. It's your job to live your life for Me in front of him. I will do the rest." Was it easy? No! Those of you that know me know I am a "fixer" and a control freak. So the "don't say a word" part was the hardest. But, for the most part, I was able to obey the Lord, and He kept His promise! So here is my advice: if you don't like what's happening in your marriage, get ahold of Jesus and obey His commands. Let me remind you, the Bible says God *hates* divorce, which means He wants to fix what's wrong in your marriage rather than have you run home to momma. The Bible says, "Leave and cleave," not "Leave and go back to momma when things aren't your idea of perfect." Let me be clear: I am not advocating staying in a dangerous situation. I am talking about letting the Lord deliver your marriage from jealousy, resentment, bitterness, anger, words and actions that have caused pain, and yes, even those preconceived notions of what you thought marriage was supposed to be. Invite Jesus into your marriage and let Him direct, guide, and teach your spirit to live righteously in front of your husband, and the Lord will win him over. Let your husband see Jesus in your life, your actions, your words, and even your thoughts. Let him see you pray, let him see you worship and praise God, let him see you study your Bible, let him see God in every facet of your life, and his spirit will begin to yearn for what he sees in you. You don't have to be the perfect godly wife; just be an obedient godly wife. Listen to and obey what God drops into your spirit. Trust the Lord with your marriage, and He will give you what you need. All you have to do is live it, and He will handle the rest. Become committed to living out God's word in your life, and see what He does with your marriage, your spouse, your children, your job, and your finances. He is good and faithful! He will fulfill *all* His promises.

Just a little side note here: Living out God's word in your life means *every day, all day*! Not just Sunday and Wednesday night. You have to live for God 24/7, not just when you feel like it, not just when it's convenient, and *not* just on "church days." Every day, all day!

Thought #82

Ps. 66:16–20: "Come and listen, all you who fear God, and I will tell you what He did for me. For I cried out to Him for help, praising Him as I spoke. If I had not confessed the sin in my heart, the Lord would not have listened. But God did listen! He paid attention to my prayer. Praise God, who did not ignore my prayer or withdraw His unfailing love for me."

You want things to change? There's your answer! Confess, repent, and praise! And watch your life, your thoughts, your actions, your words, your spouse, your children, situations at your job, and yes, even your bank account change. Seek God's will, trust Him completely, and praise Him continuously! For He is good, He is faithful, and everything He does is for your good. The Bible says, test Him and see (paraphrased). He will not let you down!

Thought #83

Ps. 3:4: "I cried out to the Lord, and He answered me from His holy mountain."

A while back, a friend posted, "If it's God's will, then it's God's bill." And I have found He always pays on time! He is never late! There's no bill so large He can't or won't pay. So whatever you have need of, know that if you are a child of God, bought and paid for with the blood of Christ Jesus, and have affirmed by the word of your mouth that He is the Son of God and He is your Savior, then all you have to do is pray; He will answer you. He hasn't let you down yet, has He? And He won't let you down now! He is faithful and always on time! Be patient! Be strong! Be courageous! He will show up every time, on time!

Thought #84

Prov. 18:13: "Spouting off before listening to the facts is both shameful and foolish."

The fastest way to bring shame upon ourselves and our God is to open our mouth without praying, without hearing from God on the matter, or without knowing all the facts. Let's not be in a rush to push our opinion or spew out an angered response. We must make sure we keep our mouth closed and our ears open so that we are listening before speaking. When we do open our mouth, we must let God speak through us. Make sure you have all the facts before saying something that cannot be taken back or causing a wound that cannot be healed without divine intervention.

"Lord, help me to keepeth my mouth and my tongue to keep my soul from trouble" (Prov. 21:23). Father, I pray that you keep me from bringing shame to You, Your name or myself by spouting off before listening to all the facts. Help me to not be foolish! Help me not to bring hurt to anyone by being rash with my words. Let Your words be my words. In Jesus' name, I pray, trust, and believe. Amen.

Thought #85

Second Tim. 4:17: "And the Lord stood with me and gave me strength."

The saying goes, God will not put on me more than I can handle. It is my belief and has been my experience that is an absolute lie straight from the enemy. God will definitely put more on you than you can handle, if for no other reason than to reveal exactly what He can handle. What's the point of having and serving an all-powerful God if we can handle everything through our own power? Put it in God's very capable hands and let Him handle it. That's what He wants! He will stand with you and give you strength. With God, all things are possible, even those things that seem impossible or insurmountable. All we have to do is trust Him.

Thought #86

Col. 3:6–10: "Because of these sins, the anger of God is coming. You used to do these things when your life was still part of this world. But now is the time to get rid of anger, rage, malicious behavior, slander, and dirty language. Don't lie to each other, for you have stripped off your old sinful nature and all its wicked deeds. Put on your new nature, and be renewed as you learn to know your Creator and become like him."

So, how do we become like God? Is it even possible? Well, according to the Bible, the inspired word of God, it certainly is possible. Believe it or not, this Christian thing came with a full set of instructions! Yep, that's right! We can be exactly who and what God wants us to be. All we have to do is read, follow, and live out the instructions. This verse says learn to know *and* become like our Creator. What better way than to read and obey the detailed instructions He provided? If we as Christians refuse to even read His word, then how can we expect to please Him? If we refuse to please Him, then we do not love Him like we say we do. If you have questions about this Christian life we are supposed to live, then open the book that will guide your life, your heart, and your spirit into becoming more like Him. Trying to live a Christ-like life without reading all the instructions is like trying to put together a swing set without using all the nuts and bolts. It just doesn't work. Oh, you might be able to make it look right, but when it's put to the test, it will, without doubt, fall apart. Build your life on the Rock, read and use *all* the instructions in the Book, and when tested, it and you will stand strong against every storm that comes your way!

Thought #87

Prov. 16:9: "A man's heart plans his way, but the Lord directs his steps."

No matter what we plan, God is always one step ahead of us, and His plans are high above ours. It's best to just get out of His way and let Him do His thing, go where He says go, move when He says move. Obey Him even when it makes no sense. Thank Him even if you don't see anything to thank Him for. Praise Him even if it's your darkest hour. It doesn't matter what you are going through; if you are God's child, you are not alone, and His way is the best way. Even when our eyes can only see rejection, pain, hopelessness, bitterness, fear, worry, or sorrow, He is there to guide you through it to a brighter, happier time. Trust Him and His plan for you. Take hold of His hand, become His loving obedient child. He will bring you through to blessings unimaginable! Trust Him; He is faithful and true.

Thought #88

James 1:22: "Do not merely listen to the Word…do what it says."

Obedience! Without it, we will never have anything. God will not bless anything but obedience. To love Him is to obey Him. If you want the windows of heaven to open up and pour out God's blessings on you, your life, your family, your marriage, your ministry, your job (or lack of), your bank account (or lack of), or your storm, then you must be prepared to do whatever it takes. Open your Bible, get to know the Person who loves you unconditionally, the Person who holds your very life in His hands, the Person who can and will bless you beyond your wildest dreams. All you have to do is submit to His will and obey His Word. All of His Word, not just the easy parts, not just your favorite parts, but *all* parts. Let it speak to your heart, mind, and spirit and do what it says!

Thought #89

First John 1:10: "If we claim we have not sinned, we are calling God a liar and showing that His Word has no place in our hearts."

Disobedience is sin. Living contrary to God's Word is disobedience. We cannot say we love God if we are living in disobedience to Him. Can we even say we are saved if we refuse to live as God commands? We cannot live like hell and expect to go to heaven. Disobedience is sin, and God will not allow sin to enter into heaven. We can talk it all we want, but according to the Bible, if we aren't walking, talking, and living it, we are living a lie. Claiming to be something we aren't is lying, and lies will find no place in heaven. So, you ask, how can we get to heaven? Open your Bible; there is a very detailed map inside. Follow all the instructions, not just the ones you like, and the gates of heaven will be opened unto you. An added bonus is that if you are following all the directions, the windows of heaven will open and pour out blessings long before you get to the gates! Open your Bible, read and follow the directions, and watch your heart, mind, spirit, and life change for the better. Everything changes for the better on the path to heaven!

Thought #90

Rom. 8:28: "And we know that God causes everything to work together for the good of those who love God and are called according to His purpose for them."

Everyone is called. God has a plan for everyone. Everyone has a purpose. It's our choice whether we step up and claim the calling He has waiting for us. We are not called just to salvation, but for Kingdom work. God has a vision and a work for your life. He will supply everything you need to accomplish His vision. Be brave, be courageous, step out into His vision for your life. The calling and the gifts are free, but you have to make the choice to accept. God will make sure everything works out for your good. He can be trusted to provide everything you need; all you have to do is submit to His plans and obey Him.

Thought #91

Second Cor. 7:10: "For the kind of sorrow God wants us to experience leads us away from sin and results in salvation. There's no regret for that kind of sorrow."

This is the only kind of sorrow that God wants you to have. People, even Christians, say God wouldn't want this, and God wouldn't want that, and that may be true, as long as it can be backed up by scripture. The Bible is inspired by God; therefore, you will always find His will, His way, His nature, and His character in your Bible. So, how do we know what God truly wants? Open your Bible and get to know Him on a personal basis. Don't assume you know what God wants or doesn't want for you or in your life. Be certain, read your Bible! Anything else is just guesswork and leads to absolute destruction! The Bible says His ways and thoughts are above ours; don't take a chance on guesswork! The risk is too high!

Thought #92

First Pet. 5:7: "Let Him have all your worries and cares."

Give it all to God and let Him handle it. You've done all you can do, and it's still hanging over your head. Lay it on God's altar and say, "This I give to You. I cannot do it on my own. I need You in my life and my situation. I need You to take care of this and forgive me, Lord, for not trusting You from the beginning." Do this and watch how the Lord will move for you. He will handle it for you and bring about the best solutions to *all* your problems. He is just waiting on you!

Thought #93

Second Tim. 1:9 "For God saved us and called us to live a holy life. He did this, not because we deserved it, but because that was His plan from before the beginning of time—to show us His grace through Jesus Christ."

People talk a lot about predestination, and in a sense it is true. It is God's plan that we all be rescued from an eternity in hell. That is why He sent Jesus, the ultimate sacrifice, to die for our sins. But then, because He wants us to love Him the way He loves us, freely and unconditionally, He gave us free will. He wants it to be our choice to love and live for Him. So yes, we are predestined. We are predestined to live out our choices and the consequences of those choices. There is no hiding behind the "predestined" clause. If we go to hell, then it's because we chose to go to hell by not accepting God's plan for us. It is because we refuse His call. The Bible says the Lord doesn't want even one person to perish, but to have everlasting life. So, He gives us the choice. He draws on our hearts until we accept Him or until it is too late. Accept God's plan before it is too late. Let Him pour out His blessings into your life. Accept His call. What have you got to lose? If you don't like it, you can always go back to the way you were.

Thought #94

Ps. 19:7: "The instructions of the Lord are perfect, reviving the soul. The decrees of the Lord are trustworthy, making wise the simple."

God's instructions are perfect, and He is trustworthy. Obeying the Lord is easy once we are free from the spirits our flesh cling to. Stubbornness, rebellion, anger, self, and pride are all spirits that keep us from being submissive to God's Word. Trust the Lord in all His ways. He can and will free your heart, mind, spirit, and give you a desire to be the person you were truly meant to be.

Thought #95

Num. 23:19: "God is not a man, that He should lie, nor a son of man, that He should repent. Has He said, and will He not do? Or has He spoken, and will He not make it good?"

Not only does God not lie, He has no reason too. He knows the end from the beginning. He knows the in-between! If He has told you He would do something, then He will do it. If He told you something was going to happen in your life, then it will happen. God's word always holds true! Whatever He has said, He will make happen! You can trust Him with your life, your family, your job, your bank account, your situation; there is nothing God cannot do! If He said it, then it is already a reality! You will see it happen; be patient, be calm, be courageous, and above all, be consistent. Hold on to what He told you, no matter what you think you see. He can be trusted to do what He says he will do.

Thought #96

Ps. 10:17–18: "Lord, You know the hopes of the helpless. Surely you will hear their cries and comfort them. You will bring justice to the orphans and the oppressed, so mere people can no longer terrify them."

God will hear our cries, and He will fix things so that people can no longer use anything against us. He will fix things so that nothing hangs over your head. Do not be afraid! Trust God to handle this and everything in your life. Get ahold of Jesus and let Him change *all* your circumstances! He will do it for you, if you just allow Him to have access to it. Turn your life over to the Lord and let Him turn over a new life to you. Cry out to God, give everything, including yourself, to Him. He will hear you. He will give you everything you need, as His child; all you have to do is ask believing, and *all* your needs will be supplied.

Thought #97

First Pet. 3:18: "Finally, all of you be of one mind, having compassion for one another; love as brothers, be tenderhearted, be humble."

There is an old saying, "Do not judge a book by its cover." The cover is just that, a cover. It's there to grab your attention or to hold what's inside together. It's the same with people. Do not judge a person by what you think you see in their life. What you think you see on the outside is what not only gets your attention, but it's what holds them together. Just like a book, what you see on the outside is usually not what's on the inside. It's only a clue. You never know what God or the enemy may be doing in their lives. So regardless of what you think you see, be humble, tenderhearted, and compassionate; let them feel and see the love of Jesus shining through you. There are many layers, many pages, and many twists and turns in each of our "books," so close your eyes to what you think you see and let God reveal what He sees, then share what He would give them.

Thought #98

Ps. 66:5: "Come and see what our God has done, what awesome miracles He performs for people."

What miracle do you need God to do for you? Have you asked Him for it? Does He even hear you when you ask? Confess, repent, and be set free. He will do what you need and so much more. If you allow Him access to your life and give Him full reign, He will cause the windows of heaven to open up for you. Then all you have to do is sit back and watch what happens. Give God a chance. What have you got to lose? Take an honest look at your life. What miracle do you need God to perform for you? There is nothing so big or so hard that God cannot cover it. Do you need a miracle in your life, your family, your marriage, your ministry, your job, or maybe your finances? Are you ready to do what it takes to allow God to perform that miracle for you?

Thought #99

Rom. 12:1–2: "Present your bodies a living sacrifice...and be not conformed to this world."

Give yourself, all of yourself, to the Lord. Commit every area of your life to Him. Everything you have came from Him anyway. Everything about us tells the world who we are. When we claim to follow Christ, but our actions tell a different story, then the world has a right to question our claim. Our speech, our actions, our habits, and yes, even our dress should all honor Christ. I'm not telling you how to dress; that is between you and the Lord. But if what we have on would make Jesus blush, maybe it's time to rethink our dress code. What I'm getting at is, do our outer actions prove what we say our inner commitment to Christ is? What we say, what we do, and how we act is proof to the world what is truly in our heart. As Christians, we must take an honest look at our lives and ask ourselves, "Do my life, my words, and my actions line up with Who and what I say I believe in?" Like it or not, we are judged by what people see, so if we wish to be judged righteously, then we must live righteous, leaving no room for misinterpretation.

Thought #100

Prov. 3:5–6: "Trust in the Lord with all your heart; do not depend on your own understanding. Seek His will in all you do, and He will show you which path to take."

Seek God's will in the situation you are facing right now. He will tell you which path to take. Don't try to understand, just trust and obey what He tells you to do. He will not lead you down the wrong path. Everything He tells you to do is for your own good. He will take care of you if you would just allow Him access to your heart and your life. Trust Him; He will not fail you!

Thought #101

Ps. 81:5–7: "I heard an unknown voice say, 'Now I will take the load from your shoulders; I will free your hands from their heavy tasks. You cried to Me in trouble and I saved you.'"

Give all your troubles to the Lord, and He will take care of them. Talk to Him, repent for all that you know to repent of, ask His forgiveness, and give everything to Him. He cares for you and wants only the best for you. Let Him take this burden from your shoulders so that you can lift high your hands, head, and heart in praise for what He has done and will do for you. Our heavenly Father loves you no matter what you do, have done, or will do. Make no mistake, your sin breaks His heart and will keep you out of heaven. But know this: even in our sin, God still loves us and longs for us to be His own. You can be free of the chains that bind you, the storms that bring chaos to your life, and the strongholds the enemy has placed in your life. All you have to do is give it and yourself to God and allow Him to handle whatever comes your way. Trust Him and His love for you; He will not let you down!

Thought #102

Col. 2:3–7: "In Him lie hidden all the treasures of wisdom and knowledge… Let your roots grow down into Him and let your lives be built on Him. Then your faith will grow strong in the truth you were taught, and you will overflow with thankfulness."

Have faith in what God wants to do for you. He has more waiting on you than you can imagine! Get ahold of the Lord, get to know Him, let your roots grow deep in Him, let Him fill you with His wisdom and knowledge. The more you see His hand, the more faith you will have in the hand you see. God is truth! God is good! God is faithful! Accept Him and let Him do what He does best. He is waiting on you. Do you not want the blessing and gifts He has for you?

Thought #103

Ps. 119:143–144: "As pressure and stress bear down on me, I find joy in Your commands. Your laws are always right; help me to understand them so I may live."

As the day-to-day pressure and stress bear down on us and weigh us down, it can be very hard to find anything to be joyful about. But if we just hold on to the promises of God, we can find joy in every situation. Did you know that there is nothing happening in your life that is not covered in the Bible? That's right; what you are going through right now has already happened to someone else in ancient times. And if truth be known, you can bet you are not the only going through this very same storm, at this very same moment. There is nothing new to this thing we call life! Even as the waves are crashing over your head, there is still a way to find joy in the storm. Joy can be found in the pages of your Bible, if you care to look for it. We will find joy in God's commands. His commands are promises waiting to be claimed! If we would but obey the Lord's commands, He promises to take care of us. God's Word, His way, His will, and His timing are perfect and all for your good. There is nothing He can't or won't do for you. Open your Bible and let God speak to you and your situation. Ask Him to help you understand what's going on and what He wants you to do about it. He will reveal everything you need to know to live a life of joy. He will teach you to understand what He reveals to you in His word so that you may live the life He chose for you before you were even born. Seek and obey the One who loves you unconditionally and live life more joyfully than you could ever imagine!

Thought #104

Isa. 12:2 "God is my salvation, I will trust and not be afraid."

Trust God to get you through whatever it is you are going through. If you are a child of His, He will not let you down. He will carry you through this as He has carried you through everything else. God gave you this mountain to prove mountains can be moved, if you just believe. Do what you know to do and trust God to handle the rest. Nothing is too big for Him, and through Him, you can do anything. If God isn't afraid of anything, then why should we be? We are covered by His blood, so everything has to go through Him to get to us. Think about that for just a moment. Let it sink in! If you have accepted Jesus Christ as your savior, then you are covered by the blood He shed for you. His blood is our armor against every attack! Trust and obey the Lord, and He will deliver your enemy to you and you shall conquer the enemy! Be not afraid! Trust the Lord! It is the Lord that gives you power to conquer!

Thought #105

Hab. 1:5: "For I am doing something in your own day, something you wouldn't believe even if someone told you."

Look at your life, pay attention to what's going on and the opportunities God has presented to you. He will only offer them. He will not make you make the right decisions. He will not make you take advantage of the gifts and blessings He stands ready to pour out into your life. Only you can make that decision. But why would you turn down God's greatest gifts? If someone offered you a million dollars, you would take it, right? What God offers is much, much more than that! Look and see what God wants to do for you. Open your eyes and ears and pay attention. He even promises that it will be beyond your imagination! Aren't you even curious? Won't you give Him a chance?

Thought #106

Prov. 2:1–4: "My child, listen to what I say, and treasure My commands. Tune your ears to wisdom, and concentrate on understanding. Cry out for insight and ask for understanding. Search for them as you would for silver; seek them like hidden treasures."

God has a plan for you. Ask God what He wants you to do next. Ask Him to help you understand. Seek His will as never before. If you ask, He will reveal it and help you understand it. Ask, listen, and obey. Whatever it is you need, God is waiting to give it to you. It's up to you to stop being stubborn and let Him take care of you, your family, your finances, and yes, even the ministry He has given you. Not that He has to, but He is waiting and He will prove Himself and His faithfulness to you. All you have to do is give Him a chance. If you don't like the blessings and gifts He has for you, you can always go back to the life you were living before you accepted His offer. The choice is yours to make. Choose wisely! It is the most important decision you will ever make.

Thought #107

Col. 4:2 "Devote yourselves to prayer."

This is God's command to us. He loves hearing from us! How can He answer the prayer if you have not prayed it? Or rather, why should He? He wants to hear it from our own lips. He wants to spend time with us. He wants us to get to know Him for who and what He is. Tell Him what you need, pour out your heart to Him. If you are His child, He will not fail you. He loves you unconditionally and will not keep anything good from you. Cry out to Him; He will hear you! First Cor. 8:3 says the person who loves God is the one whom God recognizes. Give your heart to God and let Him take care of your every need. He is just waiting on you to come wholeheartedly to Him. Commit to Him, and He will commit to you beyond your wildest dreams.

Thought #108

Exod. 18:18: "You cannot handle it alone."

When Moses was trying to handle everything on his own, His father-in-law came to him and told him to stop trying to do everything himself. Not only was it impossible, it was also impractical. I don't know about you, but I am a fixer. I think I can fix everything myself. Do you have any idea how big a mess this kind of thinking will make? It took me a long time to realize I wasn't fixing anything. All I was doing was taking the situation out of God's hands and bending it to my will instead of waiting on His perfect will. Oh, I admit I sometimes fixed it temporarily, but I have to wonder what God would have been able to do if I had not put my hand and my will to it. I have a very hard time admitting I can't fix everything. I might be able to mend it for a while, but what if I don't touch it? What if I move out of the way and say, "Lord, I give this to you. I cannot do this on my own. Forgive me for getting in Your way. Please give me the strength to let Your will be done. Help me to trust You. I cannot do this on my own, and I thank You, Father, for handling it for me. Let Your will be done. You are God and I am not"? Think about it: whose fix will be better and/or permanent? Don't you want the best answer to your problem? Give it to God and admit you cannot do it on your own.

Thought #109

John 5:9: "Instantly, the man was healed!"

When Jesus speaks, the results are instant! What would have happened if that man had not believed? What if that man had not obeyed? How many blessings are we throwing back in God's face because of our unbelief and disobedience? If God said it, it is done! If it is in God's Word, it is truth! Believe and obey, and watch the windows of heaven open up and pour out blessings on you. *Believe! Trust! Obey!* What is written will be done!

Thought #110

Job 31:4: "Does He not see my ways, and count all my steps?"

There is nothing in your life that escapes God's attention. He sees everything we do. He hears everything we say and think: the good, the bad, and the ugly! Yet, if we belong to Him, truly belong to him, He supplies our every need. Does He do it on demand? Sometimes, but most of the time it happens in His time. Our selfish nature says, "I know best when I need something," "I want it now," or "Let me have it now." But only God knows what's best for us. Our selfish nature gives us a two-year-old mentality. And if God always answered on demand, we would always have the same mentality. God does not want us to stay babes! He wants us to grow and mature in Him. The only way to grow and mature is to face adversity. If the Lord handed us everything on a silver platter, how would we see His glory? How would we learn to appreciate His blessings? How would we grow and mature? At what level would our faith be? Would we learn anything of Him? Our heavenly Father is a good father, and He is concerned with our well-being. If you are truly His child, know that He hears you, He sees you, He knows your every need, and He will fulfill each one of them. Trust Him, allow Him to give you what you need when you truly need it. He will not fail you in anything. Remember, what we want is not always good for us. This is somewhat extreme, but think about this: would you give your two-year-old a loaded gun to play with just because he wanted it? No! Why? Because it is not good for him! Because he is not old enough nor mature enough to know what to do with it or even know how to handle it. The Lord, your Father works the same way! He will not give you what is not good for you. Trust Him. He knows what's best for you and the best time to give it to you. Trust His heart and His hand. He will not fail you!

Thought #111

Ps. 16:8: "I know the Lord is always with me. I will not be shaken, for He is right beside me."

There is nothing we have to face alone as long as we belong to the Lord. If you have given your life to God, made Him the lord and master of it, then you are His child. And just as you would never let your child face anything alone, neither will He. I know that whatever comes my way, my Lord is right beside me, and if I trust Him fully, He will handle whatever it is. I do not have to be afraid. I do not have to worry. I know that as long as I do my part, my Lord will handle the rest. I have peace, knowing He is right beside me and there is nothing I will ever have to face alone. Man may leave you, but God never will. You may leave God, but He will never leave you. You can throw off His protection and never think on Him again. But you will never throw off His love for you. He will always love you and long for you to return to Him. There is nothing in this world that compares to the love He feels for you. He longs to walk beside you, to protect you, and to provide for you. If you have not accepted Him as your Lord and Savior, then I encourage you to do so right now. There is no peace such as the peace you will find with Him. There is no joy such as the joy you will find with Him. Allow Him to come in and change your world, your heart, your life, your mind, your family, your marriage, your job, your finances; there is nothing He won't do for you. He is waiting for you to allow Him to prove Himself faithful in all His does. He does not have to prove anything to us, for He is God. But for you, He will. The Bible says, "Taste and see what God can do" (paraphrased). He longs for you! Come out of that dark and dreary land of worry and fear. Come out and live in the light and truth of the Lord God Almighty. Come out and live in peace and joy! Give Him a chance. He does not care what you have done; He is waiting with open arms.

Thought #112

Prov. 17:17: "A friend loveth at all times."

All times! Not just when it's easy, not just when it's convenient, at all times! A friend is someone you can trust to always be there. They will not only rejoice with you during the good times, they will cry with you during the sad times, encourage you through the hard times, hold on to you through the storms, pull you from the quicksand of self-pity and depression, and if need be, they will drag you kicking and screaming from the darkness of your own mind. A friend will lovingly tell you the truth, even when you don't want to hear it. A friend loves unconditionally, every day, all day! This is what kind of friend Jesus is. This is what kind of friend Jesus wants us to be. This is the kind of friend Jesus wants to be in your life if you will just allow it. A friend loveth at all times! Can we ask ourselves, "What kind of friend am I?" and honestly be able to lay claim to all of these things?

Forgive me, Lord, for the many times I have fallen short in being a true friend. Lord, teach me to love at all times, regardless of what I think, what I see, or what I hear. Help me, Lord, to be the same kind of friend to others that you have been to me. In Jesus' name, I pray, trust, and believe. Amen.

Thought #113

Mal. 3:6: "I am the Lord and I do not change."

If He said it, then it is truth. If He did it, then you can trust it was the best solution. God is God! We do not need to understand everything He does. He knows what He is doing and why He is doing it. Wait patiently, and He will reveal Himself to you. Understand that all He does is for our good. Trust Him and have faith that He will bring you though it!

Thought #114

Job 42:10: "The Lord restored the fortunes of Job when he prayed for his friends, and the Lord increased all that Job had twofold."

It is true that God allowed something bad to happen in Job's life. But it ended up being for Job's good, brought much glory to God's name, and proved that God's promises hold true, no matter what it looks like from the outside. Everything God allowed the devil to take from Job the Lord gave twice as much back to Job in return for Job being faithful and true even during the hardest time of his life. This is what happens when we are faithful and true to God. He might allow something that seems bad to enter your life, but if you are faithful and true to Him as Job was, He will turn it around to use it for your good. The Bible says, what the enemy means for evil, God will use for good. Pray and thank God for what He is doing in your life, even if it looks bad and you don't understand; say, "Thank you Lord. I trust You to get me through to the other side! Thank you, Lord, even though I can't see it right now, I know what's happening is for my good. And if I trust You, I will be blessed in spite of what the enemy tries to do. I will trust You in this!" It has been said that God never sends you where He hasn't already been. So, if God has already been where you are, you can rest assured that you are safe where you are right now and He has already made provisions for what you will need while you are there. Trust Him; all He does and all He allows is for your good!

Thought #115

Isa. 43:18–19: "But forget all that—it is nothing compared to what I am going to do. For I am about to do something new. See, I have already begun! Do you not see it?"

Pay attention to what God is doing in your life and what He is trying to teach you. There are no coincidences, good luck, fate, or karma; everything happens for divine purposes. God is always doing something in your life. So pay attention and be sure to thank Him for it. Learn from what He is revealing to you and thank Him for lessons learned. God never does or allows anything in your life that doesn't lead to revelation, direction, and guidance. Everything, big and small, happens for a reason, usually more than one reason. Ultimately, those reasons, those revelations, those directions, and that guidance is to lead you closer to Him. To grow your faith and cement a closer, more intimate relationship with Him. Pay attention! What is God doing in your life right now?

Thought #116

Matt. 25:40: And the King will answer and say to them, "Assuredly, I say to you, inasmuch as you did it to one of the least of these My brethren you did it to Me."

In this verse, Jesus is talking about when we help others it is the same as helping Him. But if we read on just a little farther, we see Him talking about when we treat each other badly, we are treating Him badly. When we talk bad about each other, we talk bad about Him. When we do hurtful things to each other, we are hurting Him. Father, I pray You shut our lips against words that would cause pain, anger, and resentment. Remind us, Lord, that if we can't speak life, then we shouldn't speak at all. In Jesus' name, I pray, trust, and believe. Amen.

Thought #117

James 1:6–8: "But let him ask in faith with no doubting, for he who doubts is like a wave of the sea driven and tossed by the wind. He is a double-minded man, unstable in all his ways."

When you ask the Lord for something, do you honestly believe He will supply it? Having faith in God's ability to supply is not the same as having faith in His love and faithfulness to supply it. God owns everything; therefore, it is within His power to supply anything and everything you need or want. Of course, there are things we ask for that are not good for us and so being, He will not supply those things. But if you ask, within God's will for you, then you must believe He will supply it. Not that He *can* but that He *will* supply it. Ask in faith, without doubt, and it shall be given. This is what God's own Word promises us. If you are praying for God's will, then you have no reason to doubt. If you know that He can but doubt whether He will, then maybe deep down, the doubt comes from knowing it is not His will you seek, but your own. Also, I might add that doubt is disbelief in disguise. Do you really believe that He will? Do you even truly believe that He can? If you say you believe in God, then you must believe in His ability, His power, and His willingness to provide for you. Do not be double-minded! Don't just believe *in* God, even the demons of hell believe *in* God. You must believe Him, His Word, His Will, His power, His hand, and His heart. Do not listen to doubt! Doubt is a liar, just as his father the devil is a liar. Do not be unstable! Refuse, resist, and rebuke the spirit of doubt! Take and stand and *believe*! Trust God to do what He says He will do.

Thought #118

First Pet. 5:6–7: "So humble yourselves under the mighty power of God, and at the right time He will lift you up in honor. Give all your worries and cares to God, for He cares about you."

Don't let the spirit of pride tell you, "I got this," because you don't! If you are able to handle anything at all, it is because God gave you the ability to handle it. Pride will tell you, you don't need God. Pride will tell you, you are just fine doing it on your own, all the while you are drowning in a sea that has no shore. Pride will tell you, you have no need for the life preserver bobbing gently in the water next to you. Humble yourself, don't let pride allow you to go down for the last time. Give everything to God: all your worries, all your cares, all your concerns. He will lift you up out of the stormy sea just like He did for Peter. Humble yourself; you cannot do this thing called life alone. Let God lift you up and give you all He has for you. His path may not always be an easy path, but just like He did for the Hebrew slaves, He will cause you to walk across it on dry land in peace and in joy.

Thought #119

First Pet. 1:15: "As He who called you is holy, you also be holy in all your conduct."

You might ask, "How can we be holy in our conduct, or anything else, as God is holy?" The answer is simple! Ask yourself, "Would God do this? Would God say this? Would God think this? Would God go here? Would God fly off the handle like this?" If you answer honestly, without trying to justify anything, and the answer is *no*, then *do not* do it. It really is that simple! Remain holy as He is holy. We are not God; therefore, we are not perfect as He is perfect. But taking time to ask *and* answer honestly, then doing what you know God would do, will get you a whole lot closer to being holy as He is holy. It takes time and practice, but this is what God Himself has commanded us to be. Disobedience is sin. Refusing to do as commanded is disobedience.

Thought #120

First Tim. 5:19–22: "Do not quench the Holy Spirit. Do not scoff at prophecies, but test everything that is said. Hold on to what is good. Stay away from every kind of evil."

Let the Holy Ghost have his way in your life, and He will guide you to the right path you should take. He will help you make right choices on that path. He will help you hold on to what is good and to stay away from what is evil. He will help you test what you hear to know if it is truth, or lies the enemy is so fond of whispering in our ear. He will teach you to know the difference. He will help you understand what the Lord speaks to you and what He wants you to do after He speaks. Quench not the Spirit, for He is your guide, your teacher, your comfort, your joy, and He will not fail you at any time. He is always there to guide you; listen and obey. He will teach you what is pleasing to God. He will teach you to honor God and not bring shame to yourself or to God.

Thought #121

Eph. 4:30: "And do not bring sorrow to God's Holy Spirit by the way you live. Remember, He has identified you as His own."

If we claim to be His child, then not only has God identified us as his own, the world also looks at us as belonging to Him. So, if the way I live my life brings sorrow to my Lord, what must it look like to the world? We can say we don't care what others think all we want, but if we call ourselves Christian, then it is very important what others think of us! Our lives are supposed to be a testimony to the God we say believe in and what we believe to be true about Him. Pray that the Lord will teach you to live a life that brings joy to His heart and honor to His name. And that He teach you to live a life that when examined by the world, they can find no fault in the One you claim to live for.

Thought #122

Second Cor. 5:17: "This means that anyone who belongs to Christ has become a new person. The old life is gone; a new life has begun."

That means if you have given your life to Christ and accepted Him as your savior, you've given your old life to Christ, and He has wiped it from existence! How awesome is that? Everything you used to be, everything you used to do, say, or think are no longer part of your inheritance. You will no longer be judged for it, because it no longer exists. Your slate has been wiped clean. You are free! You are a newborn person in Christ! Everything you do, everything you become comes from God has to offer! How many times do we say, "I wish I could go back and undo that?" or "I'd give anything to change that" or "Why can't my life be different?" Well, here's your chance! All you have to do is confess, repent, accept Christ as your savior, and turn away from what you used to be. Accept the new life God planned for you from before you were born. "Is it that easy?" you ask. Yes! It's that easy! Then after that, everything you do or become is up to you. The possibilities are endless! What have you go to lose?

Thought #123

John 11:40: Jesus responded, "Didn't I tell you that you would see God's glory if you believe?"

What do you need to see God's glory in? Family? Health? Finances? Ministry? Jesus said you *would* see God's glory if you only believe. You can't just give it lip service and say, "I'm believing God for the outcome" but refuse to ask for a specific outcome. You must ask and then believe with your whole heart, mind, and strength. Let no doubt enter in. Doubt, no matter how small, is still unbelief! Rebuke and refuse to bow to it. Ask God to help you in your unbelief. Whatever you need, God *will* supply that need. All you have to do is *believe*!

Thought #124

Isa. 30:21: "Your own ears will hear Him. Right behind you a voice will say, 'This is the way you should go,' whether to the right or to the left."

Listen to the small still voice speaking in and to your spirit. Let God's voice guide you in all you do. You do not have to charge full speed into a decision that could very well be destructive. Take a deep breath and check; the voice of God will never lead you where you ought not go. Take a moment; you will feel His Spirit urging your spirit to do what's right. He will not fail you! Trust Him! Whether in your darkest valley or atop the highest mountain, God will guide you every step of the way. Before you take that next step, say that next word, or even have that next thought, take a moment and pay attention to the voice speaking to your spirit. Listen and obey. He is right there waiting to take you to heights unknown where the possibilities are limitless! The Lord is for you and wants only good for you. Do not worry, do not be discouraged; if God be for you, then who or what can stand against you? Be still, listen to Him, allow the Lord to direct your steps, your words, your thoughts, your actions, your whole life. There is nothing He will not do for you.

Thought #125

Luke 18:1: "Always pray and never give up."

Unless you know with absolute certainty that God has closed a door on whatever you are praying about, continue to pray! Never give up! Where would the widow have been if she had given up? Where would the prodigal son have been if the father had given up? Where would I be if my mother had given up? What would happen to my loved ones if I give up? What will happen to you, if you give up? Don't give up! Don't grow weary! Be persistent! Keep knocking until the door opens! Don't give up; the answer may be just around the corner!

Thought #126

Deut. 30:19–20: "Today I have given you the choice between life and death, between blessings and curses. Now I call on heaven and earth to witness the choice you make. Oh, that you would choose life, so that you and your descendants might live! You can make this choice by loving the Lord your God, obeying Him and committing yourself firmly to Him. This is the key to your life."

The key to life! It's your choice, and God is waiting to pour out life and blessings. Or you can choose death and curses. When put that way, it would seem the choice would be easy, right? Right? Then why do so many of us choose the latter? Is loving the Lord, obeying His Word, and committing ourselves to the Lord such a hard task? Is it too much to ask? Oh, that you would choose life, so that you and your descendants might live! Do you not see? The Lord is imploring us to make the right choice, not just for ourselves but for our children! And what is more important than our children? Nothing! Would you not have life more abundant and blessings beyond imagination poured out on your children and your children's children? What choice do you make? Do not be fooled; remember, by not making a choice, you have made a choice. What would you have for your children? Life or death? Blessings or curses? In the end, we all will choose. How will that choice affect your children and your children's children? And, can you live with that choice, knowing what you now know?

Thought #127

Prov. 4:24–27: "Avoid all perverse talk; stay away from corrupt speech. Look straight ahead, and fix your eyes on what lies before you. Mark out a straight path for your feet; stay on the safe path. Don't get sidetracked; keep your feet from following evil."

Don't get sidetracked with what the world says is OK! Watch what you say; whether you like it or not, the world is watching you. You are their guide to what Christianity is. It is not Christ-like to hang around and laugh at ugly jokes. It is not Christ-like to tear down your neighbor with gossip, innuendo, or malicious talk. It is not Christ-like to let those ugly words fall unheeded from your lips. Even those substitute words bring shame and dishonor to you and to the Lord. If you are on the path that Lord has laid out before you, look straight ahead, keep your eyes focused on Christ and the Cross. Do not let the world lead you; you lead the world! That is our assignment from Christ! Do not be swayed by the enticements the world or the enemy may throw at you. Depend on the armor of His blood. It will protect, guide, and keep you on the straight path!

Thought #128

Matt. 6:4: "Give your gifts in private and your Father, who sees everything will reward you."

What is better? A pat on the back from people that saw what you did? Or a quiet nod and smile from God? People may see and pat you on the back and then will very quickly forget it. But God never forgets! What is more important, more satisfying? A pat on the back or knowing you made God's heart smile?

Thought #129

John 6:35: Jesus replied, "I am the bread of life. Whoever comes to Me will never be hungry again. Whoever believes in Me will never be thirsty."

He is always faithful! Whatever you need, He will supply! If your heart belongs to Jesus, so do your needs, your wants, your worries, your fear, and your concerns. Give your heart to Jesus, make Him the Lord of your life, and you will have everything you need, He will provide, protect, and guide you. Trust Him! He is faithful! He will never fail you, leave you, or forsake you. He is always at your side, ready to handle everything you allow Him to. The moment you say, "Father, I come in the name of Jesus," you are made welcome and all your needs are met. Without question, without fail. He is all you will ever need.

Thought #130

Ps. 55:22: "Cast your burdens on the Lord, and He shall sustain you; He shall never permit the righteous to be moved."

God will take care of everything if you will do what it takes to allow Him access to your life, your problems, your worries, your fear, your job, your marriage, your children, and your finances. Is your life so amazing that it cannot get any better? Don't you want peace and joy to be mainstays in your life? Wouldn't you like to get back what you had when you had God in your life? What have you got to lose? Won't you trust Him again like you used to? Or, if you've never accepted Christ as your savior, then you can't even imagine what true peace, comfort, and joy really are. Once you commit or recommit you heart and life to the Lord, nothing will ever be the same again! Give your heart and life to Jesus, and He will change your heart, mind, spirit, life, and world! Try it! What in the world have you got to lose? Better still, what have you got to gain? If you do not like it, then you can always return to the life you now live. But if you truly give everything to Him, you'll never want to go back!

Thought #131

Isa. 41:10: "Do not fear, for I am with you; do not anxiously look about you, for I am your God. I will strengthen you, surely I will help you, surely I will uphold you with My righteous hand."

You are not alone! If you are a child of the one true living God, made so by accepting Jesus Christ as your Savior, then you have no reason to worry. You do not have to anxiously search around in the dark for answers. God is right beside you. He will give you strength, comfort, and joy. He will help you find joy in the chaos! Look up! See? He holds out His hand, waiting to help you out of the pit of despair. Trust His hand, His grace, and His heart. He is waiting, He loves you, and it breaks His heart to see you in such turmoil! Let Him in, let Him help you; you are not alone! He will save you, if you will allow Him.

Thought #132

Eph. 23:19: "Imitate God, therefore, in everything you do, because you are His dear children."

God doesn't cuss. God doesn't tell or laugh at ugly jokes. God doesn't smoke. God doesn't tear people down, belittle them, or gossip about them. God doesn't cheat, lie, or steal. If you have any question about what you do, say, or think, ask yourself this: "Would God say, think, or do this?" We are to imitate Him, not break His heart. So before we look to others' wrongs, we should look to ourselves. If we would just take the time to ask ourselves this simple question, we'll save ourselves and others a lot of heartache and embarrassment. The Bible says we will *all* answer for what we think, say, and do. That old question "What would Jesus do?" is a valid question, and the answer is "Imitate God."

Thought #133

James 1:2–4: "My brethren, count it all joy when you fall into various trials, knowing that the testing of your faith produces patience. But let patience have its perfect work, that you may be perfect and complete, lacking nothing."

Every trial you go through will test your faith in yourself and the Lord. To begin with, you must understand that He is the only person who can get you through it. Oh, we can be like the rest of the world and dive in headfirst, thinking we can handle it, without thinking of the consequences, but where would that get us? It may get you a quick fix, but then what? What if you put your trial in God's hands and let Him fix it? It may take a little longer than we would like, but it would be fixed right, and the fix would be permanent. Stay calm, be patient, and have faith. God will get you through it. You will come out on the other side with more faith, perfect, complete, and lacking nothing. There is nothing God won't do for His child, including teaching that child to grow in faith to spiritual maturity. Without faith, there is no maturity! The Bible says, "Let him ask in perfect faith without doubting and it will be given." It does not say maybe or might; it says it will be given. All we have to do is ask without doubting, have faith and patience. Whatever you need will be supplied! That is God's promise to you. God never lies! He will do what He says He will do.

Thought #134

Jude 8:21: "For as a man is, so is his strength."

If a man or woman runs after God, then that person will be godly, and their strength will be found in God. If we run after the world, then we will be worldly, and that is where our strength will be found. The Bible says we cannot serve two masters—that we will hate the one and love the other (paraphrased). Who or what are you chasing? Who will you serve? The God of all creation? The God who loves you unconditionally? The God whose only desire is to do good for you? Or the god that not only has let you down time after time but has knocked you down time and time again? There is also a god of self, but let's face it, if that were such a great god, would you be in the fix you are in right now? Aren't you tired of getting knocked down, kicked in the face, walked on, and stabbed in the back? Aren't you ready for something new? Something great? Something that will lift you up and carry you through? That something is waiting on you to accept Him. That something is ready to do a new thing in your life! Say the word and gain new strength, new joy, and peace beyond imagination. The one true living God is waiting with outstretched arms to lift you up, stand you on your feet, guide you, protect you, and provide all your needs! Choose you this day which God will be your strength! He is waiting!

Thought #135

Matt. 6:15: "But if you refuse to forgive others, your Father will not forgive you."

When Jesus was teaching about prayer, what we call the Lord's Prayer, He said, forgive us as we forgive others. So it stands to reason if we do not forgive others, God does not forgive us. Saying we forgive someone doesn't mean we've truly forgiven that person. If in our hearts we have not forgiven them, then saying it with our mouth means nothing. Forgive with your heart so that God can forgive with His. Holding on to pain and bitterness hurts not only you, but God as well.

Thought #136

John 14:12: "I tell you the truth, anyone who believes in Me will do the same works I have done, and even greater works, because I am going to be with the Father."

Jesus said if we believe, we will do the same works that He did, even greater! So why aren't people getting healed? Why aren't they getting delivered? Why are they living in pain, anger, bitterness, jealousy, resentment, depression, anxiety, worry, fear, and doubt? Why are we living burdened down by trials, storms, tribulations, and attacks from the enemy? Jesus said we *will* do the same works! Not might and not maybe, but *will!* So what's stopping us? Is it doubt, disbelief, apostasy, or just plain laziness? If we are true believers, then there is nothing, except offer salvation, that Jesus did that we can't do. If He lives inside us, then His power also resides in us.

What if the problem is that we don't truly believe? Oh, I'm sure we all believe in Him, but do we believe Him, His word, His power, His ability to use us? Maybe it's because we do not know Him for who and what He truly is. God does not lie, so if He says we will do it, then the problem lies with us. Without knowing Him for who and what He is, we cannot do as He does. Without fully knowing Him, we will continue to live as we are, tortured and tossed like a wind-driven wave, pulled under time and time again. Until at last we give up and go down for the last time. I challenge you to get to *know* the person you say you believe in. Let Him fill you with His power, His presence, His wisdom, and His strength. There is nothing beyond His ability, and by His own words, those abilities live in us, if we believe. Believe! Trust Him; His Word is true!

Thought #137

Jude 11:35: "For I have given my word to the Lord, and I cannot go back on it."

The old saying goes, "We are only as good as our word." How many times have we made covenants or promises to the Lord only to forget them as time or trouble passes? What if God's word, promise, or covenant was only as good as our own? Where would we be? I have given my word to the Lord and cannot go back on it. I pray the Lord will give us the strength to stand on this verse and live it out to the fullest. I pray that our word to Him will be as good and lasting as His word to us. Lord, I am wretchedly human and there is no good in me, save You. Help me, Lord; without You, I am nothing. Help me to stay true to my promise to You. In Jesus' name, I pray, trust, and believe. Amen.

Thought #138

Ps. 18:30: "As for God, His way is perfect."

Things don't always work out the way we plan. Usually it's because God planned something different for us, something better. Our ways are not God's way; His is much higher than ours. His way is perfect! The Bible says we can make our plans, but it's God who directs our steps. This doesn't mean He will make you do what He wants you to do. Unfortunately, we have this pesky little gift called free will, and many times, it's more trouble than it's worth. I don't know about you, but every time I've found myself in a mess, it was usually due to my free will, rebellion, or disobedience. I chose to do things my way instead of God's way. If we will commit ourselves to God's Word, God's will, and God's way, those messes we find ourselves in will become less of a mess and closer to perfection, His perfection. If we commit to walk in obedience to Him, we will discover His plans are always better.

Thought #139

Num. 23:19: "God is not a man, so He does not lie. He is not human, so He does not change His mind. Has He ever spoken and failed to act? Has He ever promised and not carried it through?"

The answer is a very loud, resounding *no*! If you are a child of God and He has told you something, the only way it will not happen is if *you* mess it up through rebellious disobedience. From experience, I can tell you He has never once failed me. Everything He has promised me happened or is happening right now. Don't get me wrong; there have been many times had I not heeded His chastening, I probably would have blocked the promise and the blessings. But He has always gotten my attention, turned me around, and has always come through for me. God does not lie and He does not change His mind, but we can block His promises and blessings by building a wall with our disobedience. Pay close attention to what He is telling you. If He has promised you something and it has not yet happened, then look to yourself to see if there is anything blocking Him from carrying out His promise. Remember, He desires to fill all your needs. Open your eyes, ears, and heart. Ask Him if there is anything left inside you that would hinder His promises being fulfilled. Pay close attention; He will answer! You may not like the answer, but obedience is the door to promises and blessings being fulfilled. Open the door and allow God to pour out His best on you!

Thought #140

Eccles. 3:1: "For everything there is a season, a time for every activity under heaven."

Understand that whatever it is you are going through it is only here for a season. Just like in nature, seasons come and seasons go. The Bible says in Job that you will be secure, because there is hope; you will look around you and take rest in safety. Just like in nature, this season will pass just as quickly as long as you hold tight to your hope. One day, you'll look around and find the storms have abated, and the crashing waves have died down to gently lap against the shore. No matter how loud and scary this storm or season may seem, remember that God Himself has promised if you will be of good courage and wait on Him, He will strengthen your heart. He will not let you go through this alone. Hold on to Him and take courage and comfort in the fact that this is only a season and He will bring you through it.

Thought #141

Prov. 12:16: "A fool is quick-tempered, but a wise person stays calm when insulted."

Lord, I pray that You would give me and the person reading this wisdom and strength to remain calm and quiet when insults and hurtful words are thrown our way. Open our eyes to see the truth of where and from whom those attacks come. Help us see past the person to the motivator. Help us to control our tongue and the thoughts that make it wag without censure. Lord, teach us to be wise, calm, discerning, and quiet, giving You time to form the words, if any, we should say in response to the attack. Let our words, thoughts, and actions be a shining example of Who we serve and what we believe about You. Help us to bring honor and glory to your name, even during the hottest of battles. In Jesus' name, I ask that You give us a forgiving heart during the onslaught and words to match it after all is said and done. In Jesus' name, I pray, trust, and believe. Amen.

Thought #142

James 1:19–20: "Understand this, my dear brothers and sisters; You must all be quick to listen, slow to speak, and slow to get angry. Human anger does not produce the righteousness God desires."

Human anger will take you farther that you want to go, hurt more people than you can imagine, and do as much damage as a Cat 5 hurricane. Angry words stir up pain, resentment, and bitterness. Once released, your angry words cannot be taken back. Oh, my dear friend! Listen before you speak; make sure you have all the facts and those facts are correct. Think before you speak, and even then, speak slowly; take your time to say those words! It is not a sin to be or get angry. The Bible says, be angry but sin not. However, it is a sin to intentionally cause pain with your anger. There is an old saying to take a deep breath and count to ten before speaking. The better remedy for anger is prayer! Let God guide you in what to say and what not to say. Watching hearts break and relationships die is not worth that moment of anger or the satisfaction you think you will get by letting those angry words fly. Pray for wisdom, be righteous in your anger, and let God guide your thoughts and your tongue.

James 1:26: "If you claim to be religious but don't control your tongue, you are fooling yourself, and your religion is worthless."

Thought #143

Luke 16:13 "You cannot serve God and mammon."

Mammon is not just money; mammon is anything that comes before or between you and God. It is true that money is one of the biggest idols we have in our lives, because to have anything, we must have money, right? What about all the other little gods (notice the little g) we have in our lives? What about the god of success or pleasure or possessions or people or any of the other things we let control our lives? What about the god of self, pride, fear, worry, anxiety, depression, addiction, bitterness, resentment, pain, anger, and hate? Don't get upset that I call these things gods. The truth is whatever we let rule our lives is our god. Anything that turns your head or heart from the one true living God is or will become your god. It might not be anything bad. It could be your husband, boyfriend, or as in my case, children, parents, siblings, might even be something as innocent as a ballgame, or any number of other things that, given the chance, will take the place of God. Be careful; the most prominent thing on your mind has the potential of becoming your god. These things become idols or gods when we make them the most important things in life. Let us not worship at the feet of idols! They cannot bring lasting change or salvation to our lives. They will only take us farther from the One who can.

Turn your mind and heart to the one true living God, have faith in His power, love, mercy, grace, and compassion, and all your needs will be met. Destroy the idols that have taken up residence in your life; they cannot bring lasting happiness, joy, peace, or comfort to you. Trust God above all others. He is all you need. Everything else will fall into place as your love and faith in Him grow.

Thought #144

Ps. 37:8 "Stop being angry! Turn from your rage! Do not lose your temper—it only leads to harm."

Losing your temper may cause you to lose way more than just your temper. Loss of temper could mean loss of everything you've worked for. Think about it: is it worth it to lose everything just to be able to spew a few mean, hurtful words—words that, once out, cannot be taken back? Is your angry outburst worth watching your child's heartbreak? Is it worth watching the person you love most walk away? Is it worth losing your job over? Is it worth watching your testimony wither and die? It is not a sin to get angry, but it is a sin to let that anger lash out and hurt anyone, even those that you feel deserve it. Be diligent in controlling your anger. Be diligent in controlling your words. Stop, take a deep breath, and pray. Let God handle your anger and your response if one is needed. Usually just walking away is the best answer, at least until you've had time to calm down, collect your thoughts, and pray. It takes a bigger person to walk away than to lash out and cause more harm than its worth. Pray! God will give you the answer or the response you need. Trust Him to handle it.

Thought #145

Ps. 37:4: "Delight yourself also in the Lord: and He shall give you the desires of your heart."

Why do we overlook the first part of this verse? Mainly because we want what we want and look for any means to justify or going after it. However, this does not mean God will give us everything we want. Sometimes, the things we want are not what we need or even things we should have. God will not give you anything that will bring harm to you. You can take it with your own strength, and God may allow it to teach you a lesson. He will not give you anything that is not for your benefit. Now that that's out of the way, let's take a serious look at the first part of that verse: *Delight yourself in the Lord.* The definition of delight is to please greatly or take great pleasure. Delight or take great pleasure in the Lord. First, you must know the Lord to find great pleasure in Him. Now this is a little simple, but then so am I, so hang with me a second. You cannot know the pleasure of eating lobster if you've never tasted lobster. It is the same with the Lord. Give yourself to the Lord, get to know Him, and develop a real relationship with Him. Without this step, there is no delight and no desire. Now for the second part: *and He shall give you the desires of your heart.* It doesn't say He will give you everything you want. It doesn't say He shall give you what your heart desires. It says He shall give the desires of your heart. Now you can take that any way you want, because that's what we do, right? He will give you new desires; old desires will pass away. The Bible says He will give us a new heart, so why would he not give us new desires with that new heart? How long would our new heart, new life last if we continue to desire and go after the desires of our old sin-filled heart? He shall give us the desires of His heart. His desires will become our desires. What He wants most for us will become what we want most. If we delight ourselves in Him, everything He desires for us will become what we desire. I don't know about you, but I cannot even fathom how awesome that would be! O Lord, let Your desire become my desire! Let Your heart become my heart! Let Your will become my will! In Jesus' name, I pray, trust, and believe! Amen.

Thought #146

Prov. 14:1: "A wise woman builds her home, but a foolish woman pulls it down with her hands."

It has been said, and I have found it from experience to be true, the woman is the thermostat of her home. If she is full of love, peace, joy, and happiness, then her home will be full of the same. And if she is full of anger, strife, contention, harsh words, jealousy, bitterness, or resentment, that is what her house will be full of. A wise woman builds her house on love and fills it with peace, comfort, joy, and happiness. A wise woman will keep others' opinions out of her house and her marriage. Even the good intentions of family and friends will bring strife and contention. A wise woman will vent to the One that can bring peace with just one word. A foolish woman will bring destruction to her home with her words, actions, and moods. Every answer a woman needs can be found in God's Word. If you need a third person's opinion, then turn to the One who will help you without judgment. Trust the Lord; He will teach you to be the wise woman His word encourages us to be.

Thought #147

Zech. 4:10: "Who has despised the day of small things?"

Have you ever wished or prayed for something big just to have God give you something small? Bigger house, bigger job, bigger ministry? Did you or were you tempted to reject it because it wasn't what you asked for? Can I tell you this? If you are asking God for bigger instead of better, you might be disappointed. All the prayers in the world will not pressure God into giving us something we are not ready for. Constantly going after or asking for "bigger" will get in the way of you being thankful for and enjoying the blessings God has already poured into your life. Jesus said whoever can be trusted with little can be trusted with much (Lk. 16:10). It's OK to ask for "big" as long as you understand and are good with Him making you better first. Take time to enjoy all the blessings while He is getting you ready for bigger things. Even Jesus started out small (twelve followers), and look what God did with that! David started out as a shepherd and became a king. Moses was a lonely old man on the backside of nowhere and became the deliverer of Israel. Do not despise the small things; you never know what God will do with them. His great power is demonstrated in small, weak things. Be patient and trust God to make you better equipped to handle the big things you've asked for. Enjoy the blessings of being obedient while He works on you. Only through obedience can God make you ready to receive what He wants to give you. And just so you know, it's probably bigger than you ever imagined.

Thought #148

Rom. 12:2: "Let God change your life. First of all, let Him give you a new mind. Then you will know what God wants you to do. And the things you do will be good and pleasing and perfect."

Have you ever wished your life was different? Have you ever said, "If such and such were different, my life would be perfect"? Do you wish that enough to let God change your life? Let Him give you a new mind, a new heart, a new way of doing things, a new way of seeing and dealing with the storms and trials in your life. Let Him open your eyes, ears, and heart to truth, wisdom, knowledge, understanding, peace, and joy. Let Him give you all this, and you will know what God wants you to do to live in a good and pleasing and perfect way. He will direct you in the way you should go. He will guide you away from the bad things in your life, if you will allow Him to. All it takes is three little words, "Father, forgive me." Let it come from the heart, and everything in your life will become new. Everything you give Him access to will be forever changed. Let God give you a new life, a new heart, a new mind.

Thought #149

Acts 10:28: "But God has shown me that I should not call any man common or unclean."

Lord, I pray You deliver me from any judgmental spirit that would influence my mind or heart when I see or meet anyone different from myself. Deliver me from prideful attitudes that would have me think I am in some way better than them. Lord, I want to see them with Your eyes, speak to them with Your lips, love them with

Your heart, touch them with Your hand. Lord, I want to represent You to everyone I meet, in a way that would open their hearts to You. Lord, help me to resist all the enemy would use to influence my mind, my heart, or to direct my path in a way I should not go. O Lord, make me clean so that I not bring shame to myself or Your name. Help me, Lord, to love everyone, including my enemies, as You have loved me. In Jesus' name, I pray, trust, and believe. Amen.

Thought #150

Jer. 17:7: "But blessed are those who trust in the Lord and have made the Lord their hope and confidence."

It doesn't say you will be blessed with a perfect life with no troubles. It doesn't say you will be blessed with smooth sailing the rest of your life. But the Bible does tell us that if we draw near to God, He will draw near to us. It doesn't matter how rough the storm gets or how loud the waves crash. If we put all our hope and trust in the Lord, we can be confident that we will be blessed with peace, blessed with joy, blessed with confidence, blessed with courage, and blessed with strength. He will step into the storm with you and calm the sea with one word, *peace*! He will stretch out His hand, as He did with Peter, and lift you high above the waves. Draw near to God and He will draw near to you. Put your trust in Him; He is trustworthy. He is faithful! He will be there every time!

Thought #151

Gal. 6:4: "But let each one examine his own works, and he will have rejoicing in himself alone, and not in another. For each one shall bear his own load."

If we would but obey this scripture, we would have so much less time to judge others. Verse 3 states, "For if anyone thinks himself to be something…he deceives himself." It is so much easier to look to others' faults than to face our own. But you know what? We will not be judged for others' faults, only our own. And we all will have to give an accounting for everything we say and do, good and bad. If I obey this scripture, I will not have time to worry about what someone else does, even if that someone else has come against me. What if we were able to examine our hearts, motives, thoughts, and actions through God's eyes? What would we see? What a bone-chilling thought! I don't want to deceive myself! I want to be able to stand before God and truthfully say I did not see perfection; I saw sin's dark stain, and to have God say, "I saw confession, sorrow, and repentance." I pray that between now and the time I stand before God, He will reveal everything in me that would cause separation between Him and me. I pray that He will give me the strength and courage I need to see my sin, confess, and repent. I pray that when all is said and done, I do not have to confess to tearing down or condemning one of my brothers or sisters. I am determined to keep my eyes focused only on the Lord, lest my heart or flesh be tempted to sin in this.

Thought #152

Matt. 5:9: "Blessed are the peacemakers, for they shall be called the sons of God."

Blessed are the peacemakers. Are we peacemakers or troublemakers? Are we sons and daughters of God or of the devil? Are we stirring up trouble and drama or trying to find a peaceful common ground to work things out? Do our words and actions add stress to a situation or bring peaceful solution? Peacemakers are governed by mercy, grace, compassion, and love. Troublemakers are motivated by strife, stress, bitterness, and anger. What motivates you? Will you be called son or daughter of God? Will you be blessed? Or will you take the other side and continue on the path away from God? The choice is yours to make. God will not make you chose either one, but He will judge the one you choose! Mal. 3:6 says, "I am the Lord and I do not change," which means you can trust Him to keep His word. You will be blessed or suffer the consequences of your actions. It is a choice, and it's your choice to make. Be blessed, dear friend; choose to be blessed!

Thought #153

Second Sam. 9:11: "According to all that my Lord the King has commanded His servant, so will Your servant do."

This is obedience! To never question, never hesitate, never fear, and never grumble. This is how we become that good and faithful servant every Christian claims they want to be. Whatever the Lord has told you to do, say, "Yes, Lord." Whatever the Lord has told you not to do, say, "Yes, Lord." Isn't that what we expect or, at very least, hope the Lord will say at the end of our prayer? Without hesitation, without question, without deserving it, we expect or want the Lord to answer our prayer as we should be answering His commands. We want to hear that phrase "good and faithful servant," but we don't want to give up control or lordship over our lives. But what would happen if we did? If we believe in even one promise God has made in His Word, then we must believe *every* promise He ever made. So, what would happen if we give total control over to Him? I'll tell you what would happen. We would be saved; we would be rescued from ourselves and our enemies. We would be blessed. We would have peace; we would have confidence in God's faithfulness. We would see amazing results of His faithfulness. We would be set free! We would become that good and faithful servant our hearts and spirits yearn to hear. Do for God what you would have Him do for you.

Thought #154

Ps. 119:105: "Your Word is a lamp to my feet and a light to my path."

When we ask the Lord, "What should I do?" there are several ways the Lord will answer you. He will answer you through His written Word. He will speak a word into your spirit. He will use another godly person, one you know has been with God, to speak through. Or even through the situation you find yourself in. You may ask, "How will I know it is God speaking?" First, you can be sure that God will *never* speak contrary to His word, *never*! If the solution contains any sin at all, it will not be from God. You can always check and confirm the answer through God's word. There's nothing in our lives that is not covered in His word. You need a light shed on your situation? Don't go to your friend down the street, unless you know for sure that friend spends enough time with God to help you find answers. Even then, check their answers against what God has to say in His word. There is no night or storm so dark that the Word of God cannot penetrate. God can and will confirm it is He speaking, if you ask Him to. Ask, believing, and then be still and be patient until you know you have a word from God. You will never go wrong if you go to the Lord first and wait for His answer.

Thought #155

Second Cor. 5:7: "For we live by believing and not by seeing."

We will never see what God can and will do if we don't stop trying to get Him to do things our way. We'll never have the amazing blessings He has planned for us as long as we keep injecting our thoughts and plans into His vision for us. We say, "God, I believe you and I know what You said, *but* this is what I think." We say, "Lord, I know Your word says...*but* this is what I want or this is what I feel." I will tell you from experience, there is *no* but! It's not about you, your feelings, or to be honest, it's not even about what you want. It's about what He wants to do in your life. It's about what He wants to do through your life. It's about others seeing God in and through you. If we say we believe God, not just believe in Him, then we will take ourselves out of the equation and let God do what God does. Our way is not better than His way, and the sooner we start living what we say we believe, the sooner we will see what God wants for us. According to God's Word, what we think, what we want, what we can do in our own power is *nothing* compared to what God has in mind for us. Trust Him, believe Him, do what God has told you to do, and let Him handle the rest!

Thought #156

Second Chron. 31:21: "And in every work that he began in the service of the house of God, in the law and in the commandments to seek his God, he did with all his heart. So he prospered."

We cannot help but prosper in everything we do if we seek God's vision for our lives, and seek it with our whole heart! Can you imagine how blessed the endeavor would be if we would seek God first? There would be no more failures in our life! No more failed relationships or failed marriages. No more failed parenting. No more failed careers. No more failed bank accounts. I'm not saying everything will be perfect or easy. In fact, doing what God tells you to do can sometimes be pretty scary or sound kinda crazy or even make you want to roll your eyes. But if we seek God's will before our own, there's no way we can fail. Trust Him; He will not guide you wrong. If you are tired of failing, seek God's perfect will with your whole heart, and stop failure in its tracks! You can do this! Be strong and courageous! God will not let you fail if you follow His lead!

Thought #157

Matt. 15:28: "Then Jesus answered and said to her, "O woman, great is your faith! Let it be to you as you desire."

How great is my faith? Is it great enough for me to be blessed with my desire? Does God bless where there is no faith? These are just a few questions this verse brings to mind. I have very little faith in myself, but I have great faith in my Lord! You may ask, "How can you have faith in something or someone you cannot see?" O my dear friend, let me tell you! I have proof! When I was yet a babe in Christ, my faith was also in its infancy. But as I grew, so did my faith. As I grew, I watched as prayer after prayer was answered, and I knew God was real and He would provide the proof to help my faith grow even more. Coincidence, you might say, and you might be right if it had happened only once or twice. But He has answered *every* prayer! He has never let me down. When a Christian prays, God hears! And He will answer every prayer you pray. As I grew spiritually, I learned how to pray within His will and not just from within my own selfish desires. As I grew, His desires became my desires. This example may seem a little over the top, but you will get the gist of it. If I pray for a car and ask for a Mercedes (selfish and prideful) but God gives me a Spark (humble and meek) instead, He has still answered my prayer, but in a way that would cause me not to sin. Just because you don't get exactly what you asked for doesn't mean that God didn't hear you; it doesn't mean He didn't answer you. It means He gave you what you needed, what was best for you. He will always answer our prayers with the best answer for us. If you have the faith of a mustard seed, plant that tiny seed, and watch it grow into a magnificent tree! Be diligent in your faith; keep your eyes open to the proof God always provides. You will develop great faith and be rewarded.

Thought #158

Rom. 5:18: "Christ's one act of righteousness brings a right relationship with God and new life for everyone."

A new life! The old one wiped from existence! Can you just imagine? Doesn't matter what you did in the past—all you have to do is ask forgiveness and accept Christ as your savior. The Bible says that what was your past will be wiped away. All you have to do is seek Him, repent, and accept Him; all that you were will be forgiven and taken away. God will remove the old you so that the new you may begin your new life with a new heart and a new mind. Let the past, everything and everyone in it go, and God will do the rest if you let Him. There will be things that are hard to turn loose—old friends, old habits, maybe even old mindsets—but if you will be patient, quiet, and obedient, even those things will be wiped away. Do not neglect what you know to do. Read your Bible, pray earnestly, assemble with other believers, and seek godly counsel when needed. Also be observant so you can see what God is doing in your life, and you will see that new person begin to emerge and your life be forever changed.

Thought #159

James 1:13–15: "God is never tempted to do wrong and He never tempts anyone else."

Temptation comes from our own desires, which entice us and drag us away. These desires give birth to sinful actions. And when sin is allowed to grow, it gives birth to death—not just physical death, but death of everything you hold precious. God will not bless what is birthed from or in sin. If it causes you to sin to get what you want, it is not from God. God will never tempt you to throw away something He blessed you with. He will never tempt you to do anything that is contrary to His word. God will never tempt you to sin. Ask yourself, "Is what I want worth what I will lose to gain it?" There are always consequences to following selfish temptation. Don't lose God's blessings just to obtain selfish desires. It's not worth it!

Thought #160

Heb. 11:7: "By faith Noah…built an ark."

Noah did not live by the water, but when the Lord said, "Build an ark," Noah began preparations to build an ark. Noah did not live near a huge forest, but when the Lord said, "Build an ark," Noah began preparations to build an ark. Noah obeyed! Noah's one act of obedience took 43,800 days. Every day, Noah got up, and every day, Noah obeyed! He may have thought, "Lord, this is a crazy idea," or "Lord, what will people think?" or "Lord, where will I get the materials to build an ark?" Noah was human, so he may have asked these questions and more. But ultimately, Noah obeyed. And God gave him everything he needed to get the job done. If God has told you to do something, no matter how crazy or scary it may seem to you, just obey. If He told you to do it, then He will supply everything you will need to follow His command. Remember, God rarely calls the equipped, but He always equips the called. You never have to worry about the why, when, where, or how when God directs. God already knows and has made provision for every detail. Trust Him, step out, and obey. Every day, obey. Be Noah! By faith, Noah built an ark.

Thought #161

Eph. 5:4: "Obscene stories, foolish talk, and coarse jokes—these are not for you. Instead, let there be thankfulness to God."

Just walk away! You don't have to be the person telling the stories, but by standing there laughing, you are agreeing with that kind of behavior. You are still disobeying God and participating in sin. How can the world tell we are different if we participate in everything they do? The Bible says, "Do not conform to the world but be transformed!" You cannot stay the same and go with God. How will the world know we are children of God if we act like a child of the world and the enemy of God? Do not be afraid! Stand up and be recognized! You are a child of God, and for the world to see it, then you must behave like one. You do not have to constantly beat someone over the head with the Bible or what you know of it. Just stand up and walk away from it. If God says, "Do not be part of it," obey Him and walk away.

Thought #162

First Tim. 4:12: "Be an example to all believers in word, in conduct, in love, in spirit, in faith, in purity."

What does the world see when they look at us Christians? Do they see God or do they see a masquerade? If they saw everything we did yesterday or even just last night, would they know that we had been with Jesus? Would they see we live what we preach? Or would they see a lie? Would they see us living and loving as Jesus did? Or would they see us living out our lives in selfish abandonment, caring only for ourselves and what we want? Paul said, "Be an example." What kind of example are you? Would a person who does not know Christ want to get to know Him by looking at your life? Do your words, actions, love, spirit, faith, and purity match up to what God commands? Do we live what we preach, or do we preach what we want others to believe about us? If Jesus Himself asked you this question, what would your answer be?

Thought #163

First Cor. 2:11: "Even so the things of God knoweth no man, but the Spirit of God."

So no man, woman, or child knows the mind of God, *only* the Spirit of God! So when we say, "God would not want (insert your own thought here)," we are presuming to know the mind of God. But this verse says we cannot know. When we say, "God would not want…" then we are putting words in God's mouth that might not match up with God's Word. If we claim to know God's thoughts for us or anything in our lives, we lie, and the truth is not in us. For the most part, I have found from experience that when we say, "God would not want…" it is to justify something *we* want. If it is not in God's Word or, at very least, it does not line up with God's Word, then we are just justifying our own selfish desires. We must be very careful in what we say. If we claim to know God's mind and we speak those claims, then we possibly have lied against God. Only the Spirit of God knows God's thoughts. Be careful to check what you think against God's word; it's the only way you can be sure you are right. Never presume to know God's mind. Check His word; you will find your answers there. Every answer to every question is in there. Do not sin against God by assuming you know the mind of God. Go to Him, and He will tell you what you need to know.

Thought #164

Neh. 8:10: "The joy of the Lord is your strength."

Don't confuse happiness with joy; these are two entirely different things. Happiness comes from outside ourselves and usually depends upon other people or circumstances. Joy comes from within! Joy does not mean that we are never sad or that we never cry. Joy comes from inner peace—the peace that comes from trusting God and having faith in His promise to always have your back. Joy comes from knowing whatever happens, you will get through it. Storms, trials, struggles can steal our happiness, but they cannot rob us of our joy, peace, and comfort that surpass all understanding. Turn to God and let Him fill your heart, mind, and life with peace, love, and joy. You'll not regret it! No, not even once!

Thought #165

James 1:19–20: "So then my brethren, let every man be swift to hear, slow to speak, slow to wrath, for the wrath of man does not produce the righteousness of God."

Ever notice that anger will turn the mildest of persons into raving lunatics? We get mad, and our knee-jerk instinct is to lash out and hurt the person we are angry at. We've all been guilty of this, if we're honest. We never, ever stop to think what our words and, many times, our actions do to other people. We never stop to think that by allowing our anger to rule our thoughts, we've set a train wreck in motion. The first result of our angry outburst is, we've sinned against God by disobeying Him. Second, we really enjoyed doing it; therefore, we did not seek forgiveness. Third, we've said and probably done things that cannot be taken back. Fourth, we've damaged relationships that sometimes have taken a lifetime to build. And sometimes, that damage is irreparable. Fifth, our arguments usually hurt more than just the two people tossing around those angry, hurtful, hate-filled words around. What about the rest of the family, children, and friends that inevitably get drawn in? Your anger may be directed at just one person, but it has a ripple effect that not only includes you and the other person but spans out to every person close to the arguers. And last but not least, sixth, it damages your testimony as a Christian. You may not care at the moment anger takes over, but who saw what you did? Who heard those awful hate-filled words you uttered? Will they still be willing to follow you to Christ? Would they even want to know the Christ you are representing? Be quick to listen, take time to pray, and think before you speak—make sure what comes out of your mouth does not bring shame to you or the God you claim to live for. Rom. 14:12 says each of us will give a personal account to God. So whose blood will be on our hands because we chose to let anger rule our heart, mind, and tongue?

Thought #166

Jer. 29:11: "For I know the thoughts I have toward you, saith the Lord, thoughts of peace and not evil, to give you an expected end."

Whatever it is that you are going though, know that God has something better for you. He wants your life to be filled with peace, and He is willing to fight the battle for you so that you can have that peace that surpasses all understanding. All you have to do is turn loose and give Him full reign. Invite Him into your situation and let Him handle it. Listen to Him and do what He tells you to do. The thoughts and plans He has for you are beyond mere human imagination. Trust Him, let Him bring peace, comfort, and victory to your life. The only reason a child of God isn't living victoriously would be disobedience. The Bible says give it to Him and He will handle it. In fact, it says the battle has already been won! So what are you waiting on? Stop asking for peace and refusing to take your hands out of it. Give it to the Prince of Peace, then you will experience true peace. From experience, I can tell you the longer you hold on to it, the longer you will struggle with it. Why fight a battle that's not yours to fight? Give it to the commander of heaven's army and step out of the way! And expect a victorious end! That is what your Father has planned for you! A victorious life lived in the shadow of the cross!

Thought #167

Second Cor. 10:4–6: "We use God's mighty weapons, not worldly weapons, to knock down the strongholds of human reasoning and to destroy false arguments. We destroy every proud obstacle that keeps people from knowing God. We capture their rebellious thoughts and teach them to obey Christ. And after you have become fully obedient, we will punish everyone that remains disobedient."

God's Word! The proud, the arrogant, the judgmental, the disobedient, and the rebellious will fall! These ungodly spirits are enemies of God and will be dealt with by Him as such. Paul is speaking to the church here, not unbelievers. If you are under attack by any of these spirits, regardless of what form they come in, know that God has your back. Don't lash out and bring sin to your door. Give God a chance to handle it His way. It may take a little longer than you would like, but I promise the method and end result will be better than anything you could ever dream up. Do not let your testimony be compromised by a rash decision to take matters into your own hands. God says vengeance is His, so let Him do His job. Stay calm, pray, and remember who your champion is and how faithful He is to those who love and obey Him. In Rom. 15:3, it is written, "The reproaches of those who reproached you fell on Me." So, if you belong to Christ, those who attack you are really attacking Christ who lives in you; let Him be the one who fights back.

Thought #168

Rom. 14:10–12: "So why do you condemn another believer? Why do you look down on another believer? Remember, we will all stand before the judgment seat of God. For the scriptures say, 'As surely as I live,' says the Lord, 'every knee will bend to me and every tongue will declare allegiance to God.'"

Yes, each of us will give a personal account to God. Every person who has ever lived, is living now, and will ever live will come face to face with God to give an account of why they said and did all the things He has not already forgiven them for. Why did you say those things? Why did you do that? Why didn't you help that person carry his burden? Why didn't you love that person? Why did you treat them as if they were worthless? Why didn't you treat them the way you expect to be treated? Why did you think you were better? Who are you to judge another? Who are you to condemn? When every question has been answered, what will you hear, "Welcome home, dear child," or "Turn away. I know you not"? Think before you speak or act. God is watching, listening, and keeping record of all we say and do. We will all be judged for our own sins. Time for justification will be gone. Will we be found with blood on our hands? Will we be found blameless? Judging by the example of your life, what will your fate be?

Thought #169

Ps. 141:3–4: "Set a guard, O Lord, over my mouth; keep watch over the door of my lips. Do not incline my heart to any evil."

Those hate-filled, hurtful words that come from our mouth as we lash out in anger is what is in our hearts and what the world will judge us by. Do not incline my heart to any evil—that anger and those hate-filled words are evil. They bring death to your relationship and to your spirit! Those words and thoughts do not come from God; they come from Satan. When we give into that evil spirit of anger, we have given in to Satan, and it is he who rules our heart, mouth, lips, and thoughts. When we give in to any ungodly behavior, we invite Satan in as our ruler; the father of all lies and deceit becomes our lord and master. Set a guard over your mouth so that Satan doesn't become your master. You will either speak life or speak death; there is no in-between. Life comes from God, and death comes from Satan. Who are you allowing to control you? Who speaks for you?

Thought #170

Phil. 2:3: "Let nothing be done though selfish ambition or conceit, but in lowliness of mind, let each esteem others better than himself."

Don't let pride talk you into thinking you are better than others. Be humble as Jesus was humble. Remember, our actions speak louder than our words. If we say we belong to God but those words do not match our actions, then not only do we lie, we bring shame to God and His name. What does the world of lost souls see when they look at those of us who call ourselves Christian (Christ-like)? Do they see Christ? Or do they see the lie we live? If we call ourselves godly people, do our words match our actions? Do our lives align with the claims we make? Would your life make anyone want to seek out the God you claim to serve?

Phil. 1:27: "Only let our conduct be worthy of the gospel of Jesus Christ."

Thought #171

Matt. 7:20: "By their fruits you will know them."

Contrary to what some may believe, this is not a license to judge others. This is the same as testing the spirits. This is so that you will know the truth. The fruit of the Spirit is love, joy, peace, longsuffering, kindness, faithfulness, gentleness, and self-control. If we are not growing and sharing all this, what right do we have to judge someone else? It would be prudent—no, make that necessary—for us to first inspect the fruit growing on our own "tree." Then, and only then, can we look to another's tree. If what you see is contrary to God's Word, then you can begin to pray for that person. Do not speak of it to others. God lets us see truth for a reason. First, ask God why He revealed that truth to you. It may be that He only wants you to pray for that person for a specific reason, or it may be that He wishes to reveal certain things in your own character that could stand improvement. Never jump to the conclusion that you know the mind of God. Get His perspective first, be open to it, and be ready to obey, even if you don't particularly like what He shows you. I have found, sometimes, the truth is a hard, bitter pill to swallow.

Thought #172

Ps. 62:1: "I wait quietly before God, for my victory comes from Him."

I've said it before, and I'll say it again. It does not matter what you are going through or what you have need of, God's got it! God's got it and He will give it to you. If you are His child, He is your Rock, your Refuge, your Rescuer, your Deliverer, your Redeemer, your Protector, your Provider, your Savior. However, if you are not His child, His arm is never too short to reach down and pull you out of the mess you are in. His love, mercy, grace, and compassion overflow the universe He created. There is nothing He won't do for you! He will fight your battles for you. He will fill you with unimaginable peace, joy, and comfort. He will give you wisdom, discernment, knowledge, strength, and courage. All you have to do is accept Him as all this and trust Him to do all this. Invite Him to take over, and all of the above comes with Him. Your victory awaits you! It is up to you to accept it. A repentant heart and three little words, "Lord, forgive me," and all this will be yours! Speak your piece; tell the Lord what you have need of. He already knows. He is willing and ready to supply every need. He is just waiting on you.

Thought #173

Ps. 62:2: "He alone is my rock and my salvation, my fortress where I will never be shaken."

When you have God, you don't need anything or anyone else. He will take care of all your needs, your storms, your darkness, your enemies. He will rejoice with you in the good times, and he will carry you through the bad times. There is no night so dark He can't find you and guide you out of it. There is no storm so wild that He cannot calm it. There is no need so great that He cannot supply it. He will be your light, your solid rock foundation, your refuge, your hiding place, your strength, courage, wisdom, and peace. When you have God as your everything, there's nothing He won't do for you. Put your heart and your life in His hands and trust Him to handle it for you.

Thought #174

Ps. 37:7: "Rest in the Lord and wait patiently for Him."

He has heard your prayer. He knows your heart. He delights in doing good things for His children. He always acts on behalf of His children and in their best interest. He may not move as fast as we would like, but He always moves! Ps. 37:5 says, "Commit your ways to the Lord, trust also in Him and He shall bring it to pass." God does not lie, nor does His Word. If you belong to Him and you are doing what God wants you to do, then you have no need to worry about whatever it is you prayed about. The Lord has already gotten out in front of it and has it under control. Rest easy and wait on Him, and He will bring it to pass!

Thought #175

Eph. 4:31–32: "Let all bitterness, wrath, anger, clamor, and evil speaking be put away from you, with all malice. And be kind to one another, tenderhearted, forgiving one another even as God in Christ forgave you."

Lord, I ask that You take away all the bitterness toward those I feel have hurt or slighted me and my family in anyway. Take away any anger I have stored in my heart against those that I have seen as my enemy. Help me to not use angry, vengeful words against them. Give me a tender heart. Help me to understand and forgive completely, for whatever attack that has come against me and my family. Wipe the slate of my heart and mind clean as if it never happened. Make this a new day and give me a new heart and mind. Fill me with gentle words, a peaceful heart, a loving and forgiving heart. Remove the spirit of bitterness and anger; replace it with love and forgiveness, and mercy and grace. Help me to forgive others as You have forgiven me. Teach me to be more like you. All my hope is in You. I cannot do this alone. In Jesus' name, I pray, trust, and believe. Amen.

Thought #176

Mark 11:25–26: "And whenever you stand praying, if you have anything against anyone, forgive him, that you Father in heaven may also forgive you your trespasses. But if you do not forgive, neither will your Father in heaven forgive your trespasses."

Forgiving those who offend us is difficult at best. But think of the alternative! If we are unwilling to forgive or refuse to let go, then God the Father will not forgive us. Without forgiveness from Him, we cannot reach heaven. Hate, bitterness, anger, resentment, and jealousy have no place in heaven and cannot be allowed in. We cannot expect God to forgive us if we will not do the same for our brothers and sisters. And what about our prayers? Do they reach the throne room of heaven when we pray with unforgiveness in our heart? We must search our hearts to see if that is why our prayers go unanswered. If you are having trouble letting go of the hurt someone has caused you, then take it to the Lord and ask His help.

Matt. 7:7 says, "Ask and it will be given to you, seek and you will find." It is there for the taking! Don't let unforgiveness be the reason your prayers go unanswered and the gates of heaven be closed against you. Ask Him for help, and He will give it to you. No hurt goes so deep that the Lord can't reach it and deliver you from it, as long as you are willing to let Him. Think about it: is holding on to that hurt worth spending eternity in hell?

Thought #177

Second Cor. 5:21: "He made Him who knew no sin to be sin for us, that we might become the righteousness of God in Him."

Jesus, who never sinned, not even one time, became sin from head to toe at the cross. Every bit of that sin belonged to you and me. Our sin nailed Him to that cross! And not only did He allow it, He chose it! He chose to endure the most horrific death imaginable so that you and I could walk the streets of heaven.

My question is, what are we doing with this great privilege? Are we living a life of thankfulness and obedience? Do we even bother to acknowledge His great sacrifice? Do we even understand exactly what He did for us? This God/man had everything and gave it all up so that His spoiled, ungrateful, rebellious children could have it all!

Let that sink in for just a moment. Everything He endured was rightfully mine and yours to endure. Will we throw it back in His face? Or will we acknowledge, accept, repent, and live as He would have us live here on earth? That is why He did it after all!

Some two thousand odd years ago, someone very precious and undeserving gave His life so that you could have a blessed life here on earth and an everlasting life in heaven. Accept or reject, the choice is up to you. I encourage you to seriously consider the benefits and the consequences before making the choice. Do not let His sacrifice be for nothing!

Thought #178

First John. 4:20: "If someone say, 'I love God,' and hates his brother, he is a liar; for he who does not love his brother whom he has seen, how can he love God whom he has not seen?"

This is what sets a true Christian believer apart from those who claim to be Christian. How many of us can say we love the person who did us wrong without putting a "but" after their name? That is what true forgiveness is all about! Christ does not say, "I love you...

but," and He does not say, "I forgive you...*but*." If we are to live Christ-like lives, then we have to learn to forgive and love without the "but."

The scriptures say, if we cannot love and forgive, then He will not forgive us. We are liars, and the truth is not in us if we say we love God but hate our brother. And if there's a "but" behind that name that just crossed your mind, then you do not truly love that person.

Forgiveness and love are hard, but you do not have to do it alone. God knows your heart. Ask Him for help. He will not deny you.

Thought #179

Matt. 8:13: "Then Jesus said to the Roman officer, 'Go back home. Because you believed, it has happened.' And the young servant was healed that same hour."

What has God promised you? If God promises something, then it is already done! Whether you see immediate results or not, believe! The Bible tells us to wait with confidence. That's because God doesn't lie. If He said it, then you can believe it.

Be still and wait on Him to finish what He started. Be strong, be brave, be vigilant, be determined! If He promised it, it is coming. Do not be worried or doubtful! Be faithful as He is faithful. He will not forsake you! His will, will be done!

Thought #180

Col. 2:7: "Let your roots grow down into Him, and let your lives be built on Him. Then your faith will grow strong in the truth you were taught, and you will overflow with thankfulness."

Nothing grows without roots. Just like a tree, the deeper your roots grow, the stronger and more stable you become. When the storms rage, those hundred-year-old oak trees are never uprooted by anything less than the finger of God. It may lose leaves and branches in the storm, but the roots hold it firmly planted in its life-giving soil. So let your roots grow deep in the Lord, and in His Word, no storm will ever rage so hard that it will uproot you. Your faith will hold you firmly rooted to the One that gives you life! Once you are firmly rooted and grounded, you will be able to stand against anything the enemy tries to throw at you.

Thought #181

Mark 4:40: "But He said to them, 'Why are you so fearful? How is it that you have no faith?'"

How many storms has God brought you though? How many times has He rescued you from the enemy, the world, and yes, even yourself? Too many to count, right? Then why are you worrying about this one? God hasn't changed! His Word says he will always provide an escape.

First Cor. 10:13 promises He will make a way of escape. He will always be your 'escape.' It is up to you to have faith in His promise and trust Him to keep it. Whatever has you worried, give it to Him and let Him show you the way out! He has not changed! What He did yesterday, He will do today! He does not lie. What He said will, without doubt, come to pass. He is just waiting on you to give it to Him and trust Him with it.

Thought #182

Prov. 28:13: "People who conceal their sins will not prosper, but if they confess and turn from them, they will receive mercy."

As humans, we try to conceal our sin. It's natural and habitual. We even try to hide them from ourselves. Like that mean thought you just had about so-and-so. Yes, that is a sin because it breaks God's commandment to love our brother.

We justify it by saying, "But I didn't say it out loud, I just thought it." But see, that doesn't matter to God. His Word, the Bible, says murder starts in the heart. Or it may be that "hurt" you are holding on to, or even worse, the joy you get out of holding on to it.

The Bible also says, forgive that you may be forgiven. Anger, bitterness, hate, gossip, lies, bad attitude, rebellion against God's word and man's laws, taking advantage of others, using others to get what you want, all these and much more are ways we sin every day without thought. And if the Holy Ghost does convict us of these "little sins," we always find ways to justify them and our right to have them.

Oh, yes! Our flesh makes it so easy to conceal our sins! Then, on top of all this, we are shocked and angry when God does not answer our prayers. If we want mercy, grace, compassion, blessings, and answered prayers, we have no choice but to take a deep, honest look inside ourselves.

Ask God to reveal what you've hidden or what the enemy has concealed from you. You may not like what you see. It is said, "Sometimes the truth hurts." And it surely does! But it is the only way we will receive mercy. Break down that wall that separates you from the abundance of blessings the Lord is waiting to pour into your life. Be brave, be strong, and be determined!

Thought #183

Heb. 10:17: "Then He adds, 'Their sins and lawless deeds I will remember no more.' Now where there is remission of these, there is no longer an offering for sin."

Gone! Wiped from remembrance forever! It no longer exits! Once you confess and repent, all your past sin and lawlessness goes out the window and is blown away forever by the wind of God's grace, mercy, and compassion. And you never have to think on them again.

How awesome is that! One simple little heartfelt prayer and *all* is forgiven. Oh, that we all could be as forgiving! There is no sin too big, too horrible, or too dirty that God will not forgive and forget if you just ask. Allow God to forgive you and He will give you a new heart, a new mind, a new spirit, and a new life! And if you will allow Him access, He will calm every storm, defeat every enemy, reunite every family member, and deliver you from every chain that has kept you bound from the life He has planned for you.

It is up to you, one small, simple prayer and you are on your way to a new life! Do your part and God will do the rest. Search for the Lord and His strength. Continually seek Him and you *will* find Him. He will stay by your side forever! You'll never face anything alone again!

Thought #184

John 1:17: "Grace and truth come through Jesus Christ."

Grace means more than love, mercy, and compassion. It means undeserved favor! God owed us nothing. We deserved even less! Yet He came to earth as flesh and blood to give us everything!

Saint or sinner, Christian or unbeliever, on the path to heaven or bound for hell, there is nothing you have that has not come from God. You have air in your lungs through the grace of God! You have the assurance of heaven through His grace, truth, and blood.

The last breath you breathe is because He loves you enough to pursue you until your dying day, regardless of where you end up. He gave up everything so that we would not have to. It is up to us what we do with it. He will not force you to accept or follow Him through salvation to heaven. He will still love you beyond your last breath even if you don't choose Him.

Just know this: everything He has is yours for the taking! If He was willing to die for you before you were even born, you can rest assured there is nothing He won't do for you once you become His child.

Thought #185

Ps. 43:3: "Send out Your light and Your truth; let them guide me."

Are you tired? Are you tired of the struggle? Are you tired of the storms that just keep coming? The waves that seem to crash over your head pulling you deeper and deeper into the abyss? Are you desperately reaching for the life preserver that seems always out of reach?

Dear friend, pry your eyes off what causes the storm and refocus them on the only Life Preserver who can bring you through the storm safe and sound. Let the Lord take care of you and your problems. It is what He does! It is what He is waiting for! Abandon yourself to His will, and He will bring you through the storm to a dry and bountiful land rich with abundant blessing. He is waiting for you. What are you waiting for?

Thought #186

First Cor. 15:10: "But whatever I am now, it is all because God poured out His special favor on me—and not without results."

Everything I am, everything I'll ever be is because I accepted God's call. Everything that I have, everything that I will ever have is because God chose to pour out His favor. I am blessed beyond measure because I seek the One who delights in blessing His children.

God's promise! But seek ye first the kingdom of God, and His righteousness; and all these things shall be added unto you (Matt. 6:33). This is not just lip service; my life is proof of the Truth! This promise is yours to claim. All you have to do is accept the call. Why would you not? You have everything to gain and nothing to lose! If you do not like who you become, you can always go back to the way you were. But think about this: how's the way you are now going for you so far?

Prov. 10:22: "The blessing of the Lord makes one rich, and He adds no sorrow with it."

Thought #187

Second Tim. 3:16: "All scripture is given by inspiration of God and is profitable for doctrine, for reproof, for correction, for instruction in righteousness."

All scripture is inspired by God and is useful to teach us what is true and to help us see what is wrong in our lives. It corrects us when we are wrong and teaches us to do what is right. It also teaches us who

God is. His nature, character, love, mercy, grace, compassion, and guidance can all be found within the pages of your Bible. I encourage you to open your Bible and get to know the only Person you will ever meet who will love you unconditionally. He will never hold anything back from you. You can get to know Him as well as you want to know Him. We cannot have a relationship with someone we don't know.

Thought #188

Eph. 6:11: "Put on all of God's armor so that you will be able to stand against all the strategies of the devil."

Satan's plan is to keep you just distracted enough so that you focus on anything other than God. Worry, fear, depression, anxiety, anger, bitterness, jealousy, family, illness, pain, job, no job, bills, or bank account, no bank account, there is no end to what the devil will use to keep you from living a blessed life. The Bible says to stay strong, stand firm, be courageous, stay focused on the Problem Solver instead of on the problem. If your head and heart is filled to overflowing with your problems, storms, and tragedies, there will be no room for the Lord to abide and free you from the lies the enemy has told you. Fix your eyes and your heart on God and He will give you the strength and enable you to stand firm against *all* the strategies of the devil. Refocus your heart and mind, you will defeat the enemy at every turn. With God's help, you will defeat Satan and all his strategies! Be strong! Stand firm! Be determined! Stay focused! You are an overcomer! You will be victorious!

Thought #189

Luke 4:8: "Jesus replied, 'The scriptures say, You must worship the Lord your God and serve only Him.'"

Do we? The Bible says we cannot serve two masters. Truth be told, though, we serve what we think about the most. Whether it be God, spouse, children, boyfriend/girlfriend, job money, bills, entertainment, food, addiction, anger, pain, health, etc., this is what we serve!

Whatever consumes our thoughts is our master. We must set our hearts on asking the Lord to set our minds free of anything that comes before Him. To teach us to let go and give everything to Him so that we may worship only Him. What consumes, your thoughts?

Promise #190

Ps. 91:14–16: "The Lord says, 'I will rescue those who love me. I will protect those who trust in my name. When they call on me, I will answer; I will be with them in trouble. I will rescue and honor them. I will reward them with a long life and give them My salvation.'"

What have you got to lose? Nothing! What have you got to gain? More than you can imagine! I dare you to test this promise! The Bible says do not test the Lord, but we put to test His Word every day. So, yes! I dare you to put this promise to the test. You will find that He will not fail you. He will always be there to rescue you, protect you, and bless you beyond your wildest dreams.

If you are a child of God and are not living a blessed life, then, my dear friend, as hard as it is to accept, the fault must lie with you. Search your heart and your life to see what blocks God's blessings.

If you are not a child of God but covet God's blessings, then your answer is way simpler—become one! Everything God has, everything God is, is ours for the taking!

Search yourself, ask God to reveal what must be dealt with in order to have all He has for you. Confess, repent, and receive, it's that simple. Call on God, He will answer! Be prepared to obey, no matter what He says. You will find the blessings from obeying God are more than you ever dared imagine.

Thought #191

Matt. 7:1–2: "Judge not that you be not judged; for with what judgement you judge, you will be judged: and with the measure you use, it will be measured back to you."

We must treat others the way we want to be treated. We must see others the way God sees them and love them the way God loves us! Not judge them for what we think we see, or we risk the same judgement from God. Are we really willing to risk the same judgement from God that we have poured out to others?

Verse 12 says to treat others the way we want to be treated. This is God's commandment. Doing things any other way is disobedience. Disobedience closes the gates of heaven, because disobedience is sin and, in no form, enters the kingdom of heaven.

Are you really willing to risk it? Is venting your anger worth it? Remember, words bring life or death, not only to others, but also to the person speaking them. Think before you speak, think before you judge, it will come back to you from the throne room of heaven—is it worth it?

Thought #192

James 4:7–8: "Therefore submit to God. Resist the devil and he will flee from you. Draw near to God and He will draw near to you."

Resist the temptation to get angry or hurt or aggravated or depressed; draw near to God in prayer and let Him handle everything. You can't change people or circumstances without causing more problems. So let God be God. He is much better at it than we are. The devil wants you mad, sad, aggravated, depressed, etc., so that he can get you to sin against God and His promises. He wants you to destroy the relationship you have with God and claim you for his own. That's his job, and he is as good at it as you let him be.

Stop, breathe, and pray and Stan will flee from you. God will handle whatever made you stop and pray.

Thought #193

Prov. 17:22: "A cheerful heart is good medicine, but a broken spirit saps a person's strength."

What is a broken spirit but a spirit weighed down with strife, anger, self-pity, bitterness, jealousy, pain, sorrow, hate, anxiety, depression, worry, or fear? How much energy does it take to hold on to these destructive emotions? In this state, we wonder where our joy disappeared to. There is no joy to be found once any one of these ungodly spirits invade our lives, hearts and minds. There is no room for joy because they take over every area and push out all joy, happiness, peace, comfort, and contentment. There is nothing left to give us a cheerful heart.

Our energy and strength is slowly and completely drained away. We ask, "Where is my joy?" when we should be asking, "What have I let steal my joy?" Search your heart, find what has made your heart so heavy it takes all your strength to carry it? Ask God to deliver you from it. Be brave, let it go! Once you do, you will find your circumstances, your situation, your storms, trials, and tribulations have no more control over your heart, mind, or life.

You are in control! You can either lie down and wallow in it like a pig in the mud and muck, or you can get pick yourself up, ask God to completely deliver you from it, let it go, and live a joy filled life. It is up to you! Are you not tired of having no joy, no laughter, no comfort, or no contentment? A cheerful heart can be yours; all you have to do is seek after the One who can give it to you.

Thought #194

Second Tim. 4:16–17: "At my first defense, no one stood with me, but all forsook me. May it not be charged against them, but the Lord stood with me and strengthened me."

There is absolutely nothing you can't handle if you trust in the Lord. Everyone you know may abandon you, *but* the Lord will always stand by you, strengthen you, lift you up, and yes, even carry you if need be. Whatever it is that you are standing against whatever attack, judgement, storm, or trial the enemy, life, or even your own sin has brought on, God will not forsake you, not even for a moment. If you are His child, He will stand behind you to hold you up, beside you to give you strength, or in front of you to shield you. There is nothing He will not do for you, if you have faith in His love and trust in His Word. Know that no matter what you face, He is already there to help you through it. Depend on His promises, trust in His love, and have faith in His compassion, mercy, and grace. He will not leave nor forsake you, His beloved child. You are not alone!

Thought #195

John 14:26: "But the Helper, the Holy Spirit, whom the Father will send in My name. He will teach you all things and bring to remembrance all the things that I said to you."

You do not have to know the whole Bible before starting to live a Christ-like life. Begin by putting in practice what you already know. God's Spirit, inside you, will prompt or urge you in the right direction. Read your Bible and let the Holy Ghost empower you to do what God wants you to do, what He wants you to say and to think. You will not become a "doer" of the word under your own power, strength, or wisdom. You may not get it right every time, but the Holy Ghost, God's own Spirit, will come alongside you and guide you to wisdom and enable you to live a holy life. Ask and it will be given!

Thought #196

First Pet. 4:10: "God has given each of you a gift from His great variety of spiritual gifts. Use them to serve one another."

Everyone is given a spiritual gift. Not just preachers, pastors, Sunday school teachers, musicians, and praise team! *Everyone!* Every child of God is given a spiritual gift. It's God's commandment that we use those gifts to serve others, to encourage others, and to guide others on their way to salvation.

You say, "I don't have a gift," but God says you do! You say, "I don't know what my gift is," and that may be true at the moment. But I believe we have to grow into the gift God gives us.

Look at it this way: you would not buy a newborn a pair of work boots and expect that new born to use them for the purpose they were intended just because you made the boots available to him or her. God and "gifts" work the same way.

Once you are saved and living a Christ-like life, God will begin to reveal your gift, and the more you grow in Christ, the more you grow into your gift. Just like the newborn and the work boots, you have to grow until it fits. There are no shortcuts; it all happens in God's timing. He is the only one who knows when you are ready to use the gift for its intended purpose. Chances are if you are saved, then the Lord has already begun to reveal your gift to you. Ask Him to open your eyes to see what He is revealing.

Be patient. Allow Him to help you grow into your "work boots" and to teach you how to use them. Let me also say: if you are not seeking God, spending personal time talking *with* Him, not just *to* Him, and spending time in His Word, it's a pretty safe bet you may not be growing. To be taught how to do something, you must spend time with the Teacher, listening to what He has to say.

Thought #197

Second Chron. 25:9: "The Lord is able to give you much more than this."

Do not be afraid to ask God for what you need. The Bible says in James 1:5, "Let him ask of God, who gives to all liberally and without reproach." God is not going to turn you away because you ask. God is not going to say, "That is more than I can handle."

Go to God. Ask what you will. He will not rebuke you. There's nothing you can ask for that hasn't already been asked for by another. There is nothing beyond the realm of God's power. There is nothing that surprises or shocks Him. He knows what you are going to say even before it has formed in your mind. He delights in blessing those who love Him, live for Him, follow Him, and obey Him. Do your part and ask believing. He is able to give you much more than this! Do what you know to do and then expect, trust, and believe that He, too, will do His part.

Thought #198

Matt. 7:20–21: "Yes, just as you can identify a tree by its fruit, so can you identify people by their actions. 'Not everyone who calls out to me, "Lord! Lord!" Will enter the Kingdom of Heaven, only those who actually do the will of My Father in heaven will enter.'"

It is written that many are called but few will enter. Who will enter? The obedient will enter the gates of heaven. Only the obedient! The justifiers, the blatant rebellious, the sign seekers, and the pew warmers will wonder why the gates are closed against them. Only those who actively seek God and do His will, will enter. You do not need a "sign" to know God's will. It is written, quite clearly, in His Word.

Be not hearers only, but doers, and the gates of heaven will fly open at your arrival! You will hear, "Enter in, My good and faithful servant." Oh, what a sad day it would be to get to the gate and find it locked against us!

Seek God, His will, and His way! It was never meant that you should be left behind! It is God's will that none should perish, but that all have everlasting life!

Thought #199

Ps. 91:15–16: "He shall call upon Me and I will answer him; I will be with him in trouble; I will deliver him and honor him. With long life I will satisfy him, and show him My salvation."

All you have to do is call on Him and He will answer you! It does not say "maybe" or "might" or "I'll think about it." It says, "I will." What more could you ask for?

Don't let your experiences with other humans make you doubt the promise. This is the God of all creation! He can do anything and will do exactly what He says He will do. He is waiting on you to call on Him. What have you got to lose? He is not man who will lie. He is not man who will go back on His word. All He speaks is truth.

He cannot lie, nor does He need to. He has seen the end and knows what you need.

By faith, believe. By faith, receive! Everything God has is only a whisper away!

Thought #200

Matt. 13:58: "And so He did only a few miracles there because of their unbelief."

Unbelief limits what God can do; faith removes the shackles and allows God free reign in our lives. Unbelief and faith are choices! You can choose to limit God or you can give Him full reign to do whatever *He* chooses.

The Bible assures us everything He does is for our good. So what have you got to lose? You hold the key to the shackles! Remove them and let God bless you beyond everything your imagination can conjure! Trust him!

Thought #201

Rom. 6:12–13: "Do not let sin control the way you live; do not give in to sinful desires. Do not let any part of your body become an instrument of evil to serve sin. Instead, give yourselves completely to God. So use your whole body as an instrument to do what is right for the glory of God."

Do not give in to sin; it will control the way you live. Give in to anger and anger will control your words, thoughts, and actions. Give in to foul, hurtful, or hate-filled language and that is what will control your thoughts and actions. Give in to hurt, bitterness, jealousy, lust, sorrow, worry, or fear and that is what will control your every waking moment and give you several sleepless nights as well. Do not give in to any desires or emotions; these are ungodly spirits, and they will become strongholds that take over your life. Do not let any part of your body become an instrument of sin. This includes your mouth, heart, and mind.

If what you say, do, or think does not bring honor to God, then it brings dishonor to Him and His name. In so doing, can we call ourselves Christian? Can we say we belong to Him, love Him, or live for Him if what we let control us brings dishonor to Him? Remember, what controls us becomes our god.

Thought #202

Rom. 12:12: "Rejoice in our confident hope. Be patient in trouble and keep on praying."

If you are a child of God who is our *only* hope, you can be confident that if you keep praying, trusting, and believing, He will bring you through whatever you're going through. Don't give up, my friend. The end and the answer is just around the corner.

The Bible says, "He hears us as soon as we begin to pray. Rejoice and be patient, the answer is on the way."

Thought #203

Gen. 28:16: "Then Jacob awoke from his sleep and said, 'Surely the Lord is in this place and I did not know it.'"

Wake up! How many times have we fought our battles, weathered our storms, or raged against the winds, only to end in defeat? When will we wake up and see that God is in it with us and we aren't even aware of it? What will it take for us to realize He is already knee-deep in the battle waiting to bring victory to us? When will we wake up and see that God is standing ready to be our shield against the storm and wind that rage against us?

Forgive us, Lord, wake us from our slumber so that we may see and know that You are with us always. That You are our Rock, Refuge, Redeemer, Protector, Provider, and Sustainer. You command all of heaven's army, and that with one small whispered prayer, You will go to battle for us.

Thank you, Lord, for who and what You are. Thank you for never turning your back on us. Thank you for your many blessings. Thank you, Father, for being in this *place* with me. In Jesus's name, I pray, trust, and believe. Amen.

Gen. 28:15, "Behold I am with you and will keep you wherever you go… I will not leave you until I have done what I have spoken to you."

Thought #204

Hag. 2:5: "My Spirit remains among you, just as I promised when you came out of Egypt. So do not be afraid. Do not fear for I *am* with you."

Whatever you are facing, remember who is with you. Whatever storm is threatening to sink your boat, remember who is with you. However dark the night may seem, remember who is with you. Whatever wolf is at your door, remember who is with you. For if God be for you, who can stand against you? No one! Do not be afraid!

God does not make promises He doesn't intend to keep. If you are His, then He is your Provider, your Shelter, your Rock, and your Protection. Trust Him and He will be your everything!

Thought #205

John 10:10: "I have come that they may have life, and that they may have it more abundantly."

Jesus did not give up all the comforts, praise, and worship of heaven to come down and live among men who hated, reviled, per-secuted, humiliated, beat, and ultimately killed Him in one of the most agonizing deaths possible just so you could live a burdened, beat-down, scared-up life! He did not come down here so that we could spend our lives wallowing in self-pity, bitterness, pain, jealously, anger, hate, revenge, rebellion, worry, fear, addiction, or anxiety. What a waste of His precious time and Blood that would have been! He came so that we could live a blessed life and live it in abundance!

If you are a child of God and are not living a blessed life, then look inside yourself and find out why. Better yet, get on your knees and ask God to reveal the answer to you.

Paul said he had learned to be content in whatever circumstance he found himself. Most of us will never deal with the things that Paul had to endure, so if Paul can live content and blessed, so can we!

Learn to live blessed regardless of your circumstances! Circumstances come and go like the wind. Blessings from God are permanent! It is your choice! Live in your circumstances or live in your blessings. But remember, Jesus did not endure everything He went through just so you could wallow in your circumstances. Do not waste what He did for you!

Thought #206

First John 4:13: "By this we know that we abide in Him, and He in us because He has given us of His Spirit."

This is how God guides us, from within. We belong to God because He called us and we accepted the call. He plants His Spirit in us to guide us, to teach us, to speak to us, to give strength, wisdom, knowledge, and discernment. We cannot have any of these things on our own. Only through God's Spirit can we have the things of God.

Thought #207

Luke 2:32: "He is a light to reveal God to the nations."

This is exactly what *we* are called to do. We have *one* job! To reveal God to the people God put in our path. It is true that how we speak, think, and act reveals our true nature, but more importantly, it reveals what we believe about God, our faith in Him, and who we believe Him to be. You cannot reveal God to the world if you live, speak, think, and act exactly like the world. All they will see is themselves in you.

Who and what are you revealing to your friends, family, coworkers, and yes, even your enemies? Who do they see when they look at you? Do they see you or the God you claim to love and worship? What light are we shining? Are we doing the job God commands that we do as Christians? Are we being a light to reveal God and His love, mercy, grace, and compassion? Or are we just a reflection of the world, shining its own light back on it? We are called to do *one* thing! Reveal God to the nations!

Thought #208

Prov. 3:5–6: "Trust in the Lord with all your heart; do not depend on your on understanding. Seek His will in all you do and He will show you which path to take."

Relying on your own understanding will take you places you don't want to go and keep you there much longer than you want to stay. When God has another plan for you, nothing, and I mean nothing, will work out unless you follow His path. You may be okay for a little while, but you will struggle making all the pieces fit from there on out. Trust God and He will keep you on the straight path. Seek His will in all you do and you'll never have to worry about suffering the consequences of bad decisions.

Thought #209

Prov. 13:10: "By pride comes nothing but strife, but with the well advised is wisdom."

Pride is a god in itself because pride is all about self! Pride causes us to put ourselves before everything and everyone else. Ever notice that "I" is the center of pride? What I want, what I need, what I say, what I do is all important to pride and self. Pride leaves a path of destruction littered with strife, pain, anger, bitterness, and broken relationships. Pride will not allow us to give unconditional love, mercy, grace, or even true compassion. With pride comes shame and dishonor to ourselves and to God. We cannot walk in pride and still call ourselves Christian.

To be Christian is to be Christ-like. To be Christ-like is to be selfless, a servant to your brothers and sisters. Notice, there is no "I" in servant. If "I" is the center of your world, in any measure, ask God to remove it and to teach you to live a humble life.

Pride will lie to you and tell you that *you* can do all things, but the Word says that you can do all things through *Christ*. Without Him, we are nothing. Seek God's wisdom and leave your own behind. The path pride walks leads to hell!

Gal. 6:7–8: "Do not be deceived, God is not mocked; for whatsoever a man sows, that he will also reap. For he who sows to his flesh will of the flesh reap corruption, but he who sows to the Spirit will of the Spirit reap everlasting life."

Thought #210

Luke 1:45: "She who has believed is blessed because what was spoken to her by the Lord will be fulfilled."

Believing is a prerequisite of receiving! You must believe to receive! What the Lord has spoken to you will be fulfilled if you just believe. This is God's promise; there is no reason to doubt. God does not lie! Believe!

Thought #211

Isa. 43:18–19: "But forget all that—it is nothing compared to what I am about to do. For I am about to do something new. See, I have already begun! Do you not see? I will make a pathway through the wilderness. I will create rivers in the dry wasteland."

It is a new day, why not let God do something new in your life? Do you not want to see it? Do you not want to claim this promise as your own? You've already started, so why not finish? Do what you know God wants you to do, so He can do what *you* need Him to do. Won't you allow Him access to fulfill His vision for your life? He can and will bring you out of that dry, isolated, thirsty land you live in now and give you all you need to live a life blessed beyond anything you can imagine. This is His promise to you. Please take Him up on this offer! What have you got to lose that you aren't already losing or lost?

Thought #212

Rev. 21:5: "And the One sitting on the throne said, 'Look I am making everything new!'"

Be brave, turn loose of the old you and let God do this new thing. Is the old you so wonderful that there's no room for improvement? Is this dark and empty life you lead now worth holding on to? Be brave, step out and except this new thing God has for you.

The Bible says confess your sin and turn away from it. God is faithful and just. He will forgive you, cleanse you, and make you whole, regardless of how bad you think you've been. Then if you'll allow it, He will make *everything* new. Your heart, your mind, and your life will all be made new. Trust this promise; test His love. You will be met with grace mercy, compassion, protection, and provision. There's nothing He won't do for you. Trust Him, His promises, and let Him create this new thing in you.

Thought #213

Ps. 51:1–10: "Have mercy on me, O God, because of your unfailing love. Because of your great compassion, blot out the stain of my sins. Wash me clean from my guilt. Purify me from my sin. For I recognize my rebellion; it haunts me day and night. Against you, and you alone, have I sinned; I have done what is evil in your sight. You will be proved right in what you say, and what your judgement against me is just. For I was born a sinner—yes, from the moment my mother conceived me. But you desire honesty from the womb, teaching me wisdom even there. Purify me from my sins, and I will be clean; wash me, and I will be whiter than snow. Oh, give me back my joy again; you have broken me—now let me rejoice. Don't keep looking at my sins. Remove the stain of my guilt. Create in me a clean heart, O God. Renew a loyal spirit within me."

Let this be your prayer for today. Let God show you what He has in store for you. He won't give it unless you ask for it.

Thought #214

Eph. 3:20: "Now all glory to God, who is able, through His mighty power at work within us, to accomplish infinitely more that we might ask or think."

How often do we limit God with our prayers? If we believe in Him, His word, and His promises, then should we not pray our prayer then ask for His will be done, not ours?

The Bible says, ask and you shall receive, but the more I think about it, I think I would rather talk to Him about it, then ask Him to do what He pleases in my life. He says He can do more than I can ask or think. So yes, Lord, you know my heart for this situation and what I've asked for, but please, Jesus, don't let my prayers limit what You want to do. Your will be done, Lord. In Jesus's name, I pray, trust, and believe. Amen.

Thought #215

Ps. 119:105–107: "Your word is a lamp to guide my feet and a light for my path. I've promised it once, and I'll promise it again: I will obey Your righteous regulations. I have suffered much, O LORD: restore my life again as You promised."

Is the life you have right now worth what you are going through to keep it? Are you sick and tired of the life you have right now? Nothing going right, no money, bills you can't pay, constantly fighting with your spouse or family, always being angry, worried, afraid, bitter, jealous—what kind of life is that?

Confess, repent, and ask God for a new life! He will give it to you, if you ask for it! Stop sitting there doing nothing and wishing something would happen! Do what you know to do and then ask God to do the rest. It's not what God wants, but He will allow you to do the same thing over and over and over! He doesn't want to, but He will let you sit there and spin your wheels like a car stuck in a mud bog. Maybe you should ask yourself why. Why would you do that, when all it takes to get out of the mud is to ask for help from the One that has promised not only to pull you out, but to also wash *all* the mud away and make everything clean and new.

Thought #216

Ezek. 18:31: "Put all your rebellion behind you and find yourselves a new heart and a new spirit."

Living a Christ-like life is easier than you think. The Bible is your guide. If the Bible says to do it, then do it. If it says don't do it, then don't! Aside from the animal sacrifices, that are no longer required, God's word is the same yesterday, today, and forever. You can trust every word!

Thought #217

First Cor. 6:19–20: "You are not your own…, you were bought with a price."

Do you not see how much God loves you? What an awful price to pay for such ungrateful children! But He paid it with no thought to the pain and humiliation He would have to endure, with unconditional love and with full knowledge that some would throw it back in His face. He paid that price so we would not have to. Would you be willing to pay the same price for someone that didn't care? Someone so ungrateful they would throw this priceless gift back in your face? No? To be honest, I would not! But thankfully, He is not me! He knew and He still allowed them (us) to do the most horrific things to Him! Oh yes, it was us! Because if not for us, then everything He went through would not have been necessary! I put Him there! You put Him there! We hammered each nail into Him! I drove the spear into Him that drained His life blood away! And all the while He prayed for my forgiveness! Oh yes, on that day, my soul was bought and paid for, even as I stood there watching Him die. Yes, it was me! Yes, it was you! What have we done with this precious and priceless gift? Have we surrendered our life to Him? True surrender? Complete surrender?

Thought #218

Matt. 5:14: "You are the light of the world—like a city on a hilltop that cannot be hidden."

Whose path are you lighting, and where will it lead them? Will it lead them to the throne room of heaven or deeper into darkness? Are your words and actions helping someone on the path to God? Or do they so closely match the world's words and actions that the path you light leads to hell? The Bible teaches us to be a living example. What kind of example are we living? Is it Christ-like or worldly? Where will that person watching you end up by following your example?

Thought #219

Mark 2:8: "Jesus knew immediately what they were thinking, so He asked them, 'Why do you question this in your hearts?'"

How many times has our doubt delayed or even blocked what God wanted to do for us? We know God cannot lie. So if God has promised and we are not receiving, then it must be *us* that has delayed or blocked the promise. I encourage you to rebuke and refuse to tolerate the spirits of doubts, worry, fear, and confusion in your life. These are not from God! What God promised will happen if you but trust and believe with your heart, mind, and strength. It *will* happen! Do not question how, why, or when. Just believe!

Thought #220

Eph. 4:27: "Nor give place to the devil."

This verse is short and admittedly part of a bigger verse, but this part pricked my heart this morning. It was speaking to the prayer I had just finished praying. "Nor give place to the devil." What a powerful statement! As I paused to think about this verse, a question formed in my mind: "Where have I given place to the devil?" My answers were doubt, worry, and fear. Your answers may be the same or different, but my answers brought to mind the verses about leaven. And in that moment, I saw truth! I have given place to the devil through my doubt, my fear, and my worry over things I have no control over. And just like with the leaven, if I don't confess, repent, and turn away from these dark spirits, they will invade every area of my life. They will grow and become my gods.

I will not let my enemy defeat me! My God is able and will deliver me from the *place* I've given in to. What *place* have you given to the enemy? How much leaven has he already added to that place? Give it to God, leave it with Him, and let Him deliver you. Search your heart; find all the places you've let your enemy reign. Commit it to the Lord and He will give you freedom. That *place* will never control your heart, mind, or life again.

In Jesus's name, I claim this for you and for myself! My God is greater than my *place* and my enemy! In the name of Christ Jesus, I rebuke my enemy, the devil, and all the ungodly spirits I have let invade my heart, mind, and life. I refuse to let my enemy defeat me, even if that enemy is myself! I am a child of God, and I refuse to let my enemy defeat what the blood of Jesus has given victory to. In the name of Jesus, I am forgiven and set free of the "places" I once had given to the devil. In Jesus's name I pray, trust, and believe. Amen!

Thought #221

Gal. 5:16: "I say then: walk in the Spirit, and you shall not fulfill the flesh."

If we would let the Spirit direct our tongue, there would never be a reason to say, "I'm sorry." We would never have to apologize! We would never have to ask forgiveness. If we would let the Spirit direct our thoughts, we'd never judge another person by what we think we see in them. There would only be love, mercy, and compassion for our fellow man. If we would let the Spirit direct our lives, no one would ever lack anything, make bad decisions, be bitter, live in anger, look for ways to "get back" at someone. There'd be no gossip, no hateful speech, no division, no racism, no way anyone could turn us against each other. There'd be no prisons, physical or spiritual.

If we'd walk in the Spirit, the Spirit would rule our words, our thoughts, and our actions. If we'd walk in the Spirit, hell would not have to expand its borders even an inch more. If we walk in the Spirit, our enemy becomes our friend, and the enemy of God would no longer have a door in which to enter our lives. If we let the Spirit direct our lives, the desires of our human nature will no longer rule us. The Spirit will act on our behalf, and those desires will not consume our thoughts, actions, or words. You say, "I can't live without sinning!" or, "Everyone sins," and you'd be right. But the Bible plainly states that we don't have to! This verse is one of many, but it says that if we walk in the Spirit, we will not fulfill the lusts of the flesh. What is lust but sin? Commit yourself to walk in the Spirit for at least one day then look back at your day and see how much less sin was there. Commit yourself to the Lord and He will help you obey His command. You can't do it on your own. Depend on Christ's power to help you, He will enable you to do all He asks of you.

Thought #222

First Cor. 6:19–20: "Or do you not know that your body is the temple of the Holy Spirit who is in you, whom you have from God, and you are not your own? For you were bought at a price; therefore glorify God in your body and in your spirit, which are God's."

Lord, my body is Your temple. Teach me, Lord, to treat it as such. Help me, Father, teach me to clean it up inside and make it holy so that Your Holy Spirit is comfortable living in it. Teach me to dress the outside so that the world knows it and I belong to You. Lord, make my spirit a roommate You can abide in peace with so that there be no strife between Your Spirit and mine. Let not the price You paid be in vain. Remove my rebellious nature and replace it with Your own. Your Word says we are called by Your name. Teach me Your ways and plant Your word and Your Spirit in my heart so that my body, my words, my thoughts, and my actions bring honor to Your name. I am Yours, Lord, do with me as You will. In Jesus's name I pray, trust, and believe. Amen.

Thought #223

Dan. 10:19: "And he said, 'O man, greatly beloved, fear not! Peace be to you; be strong, yes, be strong!'"

You are very precious to God. Be encouraged! Think about how precious your family is to you. Think about how much you love them and what you would do for them, what lengths would you go? Is there anything you wouldn't do for them? Now multiply that by an unimaginable number and that's how precious you are to God. If you say there is no limit to what you would do for your loved ones, how much more will your heavenly Father do for you? Trust Him, He loves you and wants what's best for you. He will give you strength and peace if you will but trust Him.

Thought #224

Luke 6:37: "Judge not, and you shall not be judged. Condemn not, and you shall not be condemned. Forgive and you will be forgiven."

Don't judge others and God will have less to judge you for. Forgive others and God will forgive you. Treat others the way you want God to treat you. Bless others the way you want God to bless you. Help others the way God helps you. Speak to and about others the way you want God to speak to and about you. Love others the way God loves you. Even those that judge you, attack you, lie to you, lie about you, and hate you, yes, even those!

Jesus did not condemn us to hell because we did all this and more to Him. If we are to be Christian (Christ-like), then we must do as He did and still does. We say, "But it's not that easy." Really? Do you think it was easy for Him to leave heaven, enter this dark, dreary, ungrateful world? Do you think it was easy to endure the whip, the pain, the weight of the cross after the beating, the sin heaped on His shoulders, the spear shoved in His side? Do you think it was easy for Him to pray for us as He took His last breath? No, of course not! But He did it and so must we, if we want to enter through the gates of heaven and hear Him say, "Well done, my good and faithful servant." The alternative is to choose hell. It is a choice; it is your choice. Which will you choose?

Thought #225

Matt. 6:33: "Seek the Kingdom of God above all else and live righteously and He will give you everything you need."

There is nothing beyond God's ability. He will give you everything you need, if you obey Him. All He asks is that you seek Him above all else and to live righteously. If you obey the first command, the second command will come as a result of the first. You cannot have one without the other. You cannot seek God with all your heart and remain unchanged! Seek God and everything else will fall into place.

Thought #226

John 16:33: "I have told you all this so that you may have peace in Me. Here on earth you will have many trials and sorrows. But take heart, because I have overcome the world."

Do you want peace in whatever it is you are dealing with? Do you want the winds to stop howling? Do you want the waves to stop crashing over your head? Do you want fear to disappear? Do you want stress to stop being the controlling factor in your life? Then *stop* giving it the power to control you. All these are tactics of the enemy to distract you from the peace God has already granted you. Jesus said, "I have overcome the world." That means He has already fought every battle for you, *before* the battle ever began. Take heart! Peace is yours for the taking! Give that trial or sorrow to God and let Him handle it! Pray, give, and receive, then leave it alone! Once you give it to God, it is no longer your problem. You gave it to God, now it's His responsibility, let Him handle it!

Thought #227

Matt. 9:29: "Then He touched their eyes and said, 'According to your faith let it be to you.'"

Hold on to what God has told you! No matter how long it takes, hold on! God does not lie! Because of your faith it will happen! Do not look at what it looks like, look at the One who told you what would happen. Get your eyes off your situation and believe God. If you are His, then whatever it is has already been taken care of! Believe God! How much faith do you have? Hold on, believe God and watch miracles happen!

Thought #228

Rom. 2:28–29: "For he is not a Jew who is one outwardly, nor is circumcision that which is outward in the flesh; but he is a Jew who is one inwardly, in the Spirit, not in the letter, whose praise is not from men but from God."

Since I am not Jewish, I am going to switch out a word or two in this verse so that it applies to myself. Yes! We can and should do this!

For she is not a Christian who is one outwardly, nor is circumcision that which is outward in the flesh; but she is a Christian who is one inwardly, in the Spirit, not in the letter, whose praise is not from men but from God.

It is true that we are to be set apart so that the world can "see" that we belong to Christ. But "seeing" isn't everything. What good does it do me, you, or anyone else if we just look the part? If I am not Christian (Christ-like) on the inside as well as on the outside, I am living a lie, and the Truth is not in me. If I have not allowed the Lord to circumcise, cut away, the useless part of my flesh, what good am I to His kingdom, His purpose, or His vision? What harm, dishonor, and shame will I bring to His name if all my "Christianity" is on the outside?

Oh, I may get praise from man, because we see the outside first. But after a while, the truth would show through and man would begin to see what God sees. If I look the part but my heart does not belong to God, my fruit is rotten, and my life is a lie. I may get made fun of, looked down on or attacked for being who I am, but I'd rather have my Lord's praise than man's applause. How about you?

Thought #229

First Thess. 5:19–22: "Do not quench the Spirit. Do not despise prophecies, but test all things. Hold fast to what is good. Abstain from every kind of evil."

Man of God, woman of God, are you where you used to be? Are you still on fire for God? Are you still filled with that unquenchable desire to get close to Him? To know Him? To feel Him? To hear from Him? Has life gotten in the way? Has the enemy distracted you? Do you wish you could go back to that place where you were in love with God?

Open your Bible! Start praying the way you used to pray! Grab hold of God and hold on tight. Stop refusing what God wants to give you, do not be afraid! You know the difference between what God wants for you and what you want. You know what God considers evil, stay away from *every* kind of evil. If it's not something Jesus would say or do, consider it evil and stop doing it! Rebuke, resist, recover, and restore! The One who loves you more than He loved life is waiting right where you left Him. He is waiting with open arms for you, His beloved child.

Thought #230

Rom. 8:38: "And I am convinced that noting can ever separate us from God's love. Neither death nor life, neither angels nor demons, neither our fears for today nor our worries for tomorrow—not even the powers of hell can separate us from God's love."

This does not mean we can do anything we want or that we can live like hell and still go to heaven. But it does mean that even if we stumble, even if we fall, God is right there to pick us up, dust us off, and help us to get back on the path again. You can never fall so far that God cannot reach down and pick you up. Trust Him! He will either lift you out of your circumstances or walk through them with you. He will give your strength, comfort, and peace if you let Him.

Thought #231

First Tim. 1:7: "For God has not given us a spirit of fear, but of power and of love and of sound mind."

God does not and will not give you a spirit of fear! If you are entertaining a spirit of fear, then you have accepted a gift from the enemy. It is a twofold gift: it comes with torment. If you allow fear to stay, it will torment and control your every thought and action. I speak from experience on this. This is not what God wants for you. That is why His gifts include *power*, power to resist the enemy and the ungodly spirits that he brings with him; *love*, love to overcome the spirits that come with those the enemy would use against us; *sound mind*, a sound mind to know the difference between misguided people and truly wicked people. A sound mind to know when something or someone is from God and when it is not. You do not have to live with a spirit of fear or any other spirit not sent from God.

Accept God's gifts and you will have the power, wisdom, and knowledge to know how to live as He intends for you to live. Seek Him out and ask for what you need and expect Him to deliver. Live by, love, and obey His commands and the enemy will have no hold on you. You will be able to resist, rebuke, and remove all the enemy's attempts to set up strongholds in your life, heart, and mind. You will live a life of power, love, and sound mind.

Thought #232

Mic. 7:7: "As for me, I look to the Lord for help. I wait confidently for God to save me, and my God will certainly hear me."

God knows your need before you even ask. He is just waiting on you to bring it to Him. His power to fill this need is beyond your imagination. You can be confident He is able to do much more that you can ask or think. Bring your need, regardless of how big it is and lay it at His feet. Set no limit on Him, be patient, and watch what He can and will do for you.

Thought #233

Job 2:10: "Shall we accept good from God and not trouble?"

We have become a society of overindulged, spoiled human beings! What do you think we would be like if all that came our way was abundant blessings? Can you imagine what we'd be like if we never faced trouble, trials, or storms? While it may seem wonderful to go through life with no troubles at all, how would we learn faith in a life like that?

If everything were always perfect, what need would there be for God? Paul mentions being happy in whatever circumstances we find ourselves in, and isn't that what we really want? To be happy? To find joy in all things? Everything does not have to be perfect for you to be filled with joy. Happiness, peace, and joy come from within. Nothing external brings lasting joy! Without God, without trouble, without sorrow, how would we know true happiness or peace or joy? If you are not happy or at peace in your spirit, you have nothing. God will not bring trouble on you, but He will allow you to do it to yourself so that you will come to know Him, His peace, and His joy.

Learn to be happy in all seasons. For when you fall into trouble, it will be God and your faith that bring you out. When you depend on your faith in God, trouble is, nothing more than lessons learned. When troubles come, lean on your Savior and trust He will bring you through. Let the Lord perfect your faith and trust that this will bring the perfect life you are waiting and wishing for.

Thought #234

Phil. 4:7: "And the peace of God which surpasses all understanding will guard your hearts and minds through Christ Jesus."

Are you living with this kind of peace? Are you looking for this kind of peace? Did you know it even existed? Call out to God and it can be yours. However, *you* have to be willing to accept it. You have to be willing to give up whatever it is that has you in bondage. Because let's face it, if you weren't in bondage, if you could have given yourself over to peace, then you would not be in this shape. I speak from experience!

For years I cried out to God, "Give me peace, I really need Your peace, please, God, give me peace!" I couldn't understand why God wasn't answering my prayer! Then one day I heard a whisper in my spirit telling me I had no peace because I refused to give up the very thing that caused my chaos. I was not willing to give God what caused my fear, my anxiety, my confusion, my anger, and yes, even my bitterness.

I thought I had, I told myself I had, I even told God I had, but in reality, all I had done was offer my fear, anxiety, confusion, regret, anger, and bitterness. But I would not relinquish my control of the very thing that caused all those emotions. The "root" of those problems I held to in a tight death grip. I just couldn't give up control. But then I begin to see I wasn't in control, I was in bondage! Once I allowed God to reveal what I was doing, I could see the chains wrapped around my heart, my mind, and in all honesty, my entire life. If you truly want God's peace, then do not give God your symptoms, give Him the "root." Then and only then will you experience His peace. I promise it exceeds anything you could ever imagine!

Thought #235

First Cor. 11:31: "For if we would judge ourselves, we would not be judged."

Before we presume to judge others, we must, first, honestly and righteously judge ourselves. The Bible says, we must remove the log from our own eye before thinking ourselves qualified to do surgery on our brother or sister. It also teaches us that if we judge them, we will also be judged. If we condemn them, then we too are condemned by the same measure. So the question that begs the answer is simply this: is it worth it?

The Bible leaves no doubt that if we are judged, we will all fall short. It would be better that we spend our time judging ourselves rather than someone else. Because, sooner or later, we will all stand in judgement for, not what someone else did, but our own actions. On that day, it will not be another man that judges us. It will be the only One qualified to judge anyone. So before judging another, take a peek at yourself through God's eyes and see what He sees. If we do this, then there will be no time or inclination left to judge anyone else.

Thought #236

Prov. 21:30: "There is no wisdom or understanding or counsel against the Lord."

There is no wisdom, no insight, no plan that can succeed against God. Everything and everyone the enemy has ever used against you will come to nothing. The reason Jesus came to earth was to destroy the work of the devil. Open your eyes to follow God! If you be on His side, you will have all you need. God's provision does not have a limit. All you need is exactly what God wants to provide. Everything the enemy has used against you God will use for your good! Follow Him, trust Him, rely solely on Him, and you will lack nothing! The choice is yours, He will not force you. Come to Him and everything He has becomes yours for the taking. What more could you ask?

Thought #237

Luke 8:17: "For all that is secret will eventually be brought into the open and everything that is concealed will be brought to light and made known to all."

This is another promise from God everyone can depend on. Whether deeds are "good" or "dirty," it matters not. Nothing is hidden forever. Everything will be brought to light and made known to all! Make sure all your deeds are "good"! Facing the consequences of good deeds will be much better than facing consequences of dirty deeds and much less embarrassing when brought to light. If you call yourself Christian, then keep all your deeds good and worthy to be called Christ-like. Do not grieve God's Spirit with anything less.

Thought #238

Acts 16:7: "But again the Spirit did not allow them to go there."
Shhhhh! Listen quietly. Do you hear it? That gentle voice saying, *Yes, go here. No, that's not for you. Yes, speak to that person. No, now is not the time. Wait, that is not in My plans for you.*

God speaks, and He speaks to you! Listen quietly and you will hear Him speaking, guiding, whispering His love and guidance to you. You will hear a quiet voice in your spirit and know that it is He who speaks. He will never leave you to figure things out on your own. He is always there to direct you in the way you should go. This is His promise to us. All we have to do is sit quietly in His presence and He will speak.

Thought #239

First Cor. 10:13: "No temptation has overtaken you except such as is common to man; but God is faithful, who will not allow you to be tempted beyond what you are able, but with the temptation will also make a way of escape, that you may be asked to bear it."

People say, "God will never put more on me than I can handle." My first thought is, really? If that be so, then why would you even need God? It is God's desire that we love Him with our whole heart, mind, and strength, and to rely on Him wholeheartedly. If we can get through things on our own, then there is no need to rely on God. That's not what this scripture really says! Look closer! It says, He will not allow you to be tempted beyond what you are able without giving you an escape. He is the escape!

God will never put more on you than you can handle with Him at your side. There is rarely a way out without Him. Take advantage of His offer. Whatever you are going through or seem to be stuck in, look to God for your way out. Your situation is not permanent if you will allow God to be your way out! With God, this storm that's about to pull you under is only a blip on your radar. Turn this temporary situation into a permanent solution. God is your way out, what are you waiting on? Take it! Trust Him and watch that storm disappear beyond the horizon.

Thought #240

Second Tim. 1:7: "For God has not given us a spirit of fearfulness, but one of power, love, and sound judgement."

The only fear God encourages in a Christian's life is the fear/respect of God. Our worldly fear keeps us from pleasing God. Fear causes us to question what God has clearly told us to do and we doubt whether we heard Him correctly. Fear is no excuse for disobedience. There is no reason to live in fear when we have the mighty presence of the Holy Ghost living inside us! God's got this, let God do what God does best and don't be afraid!

Thought #241

Acts 21:14: "We gave up and said, 'The Lord's will be done.'"

What is it that you need to give up? What has you so worried it consumes your thoughts? What, at the mere thought of it, throws you into a panic or rage? What has become so big it's taken over your life and has come between you and God? Do you think it too big for God to handle? Or, as with most of us, is it because you don't think He will handle it the way you think it ought to be handled? Or maybe you've become so use to the pit of misery you live in, you're afraid to give it up? Give it up! Nothing is too big for God and nothing, absolutely nothing is worth losing contact with the presence of God. Give it up, give it to God, find peace, deliverance, and redemption! Let your heart, mind, body, and soul rest in the peace that only comes from letting God handle it.

Thought #242

Luke 9:23: "Take up your cross daily and follow me."

That means if we want to be a follower of Christ, we must give up our way, take up our cross (His way), and follow Him, His wishes, His way.

What the "old" you wanted to say or do or think has nothing to do with the "new" you. Before you act, think, or speak, ask yourself, is this His way? Would Jesus say this? Would He think this? Would He act like this? Would He go here? Taking on the cross of Jesus is to take on His way, His nature, His very character! Think before you speak or act and remember Who you represent. There are only two choices: Jesus or His enemy, the devil. It cannot be both. You will act like one or the other. Who do you choose to represent?

Thought #243

Gen. 3:10: "I heard You in the garden and I was afraid."

All fear is bondage, with the exception of "fear of the Lord." Fear says we don't trust God. Fear comes between us and what God wants for us. Fear will steal trust, love, mercy, and compassion. Fear will steal your life. Fear does not come from God!

The Bible says, we are not given a spirit of fear. So then, where does it come from? It comes from the enemy of your heart, mind, and soul. Fear is a liar, a thief, and a murderer. God has not given you a spirit of fear but of love and of power. Accept and trust what God has given you and defeat what the enemy intends for you. God is always with you. He is your Rock, your Shield, your Provider, your Savior. There is nothing He won't do for you. Trust Him, lean on His strength, His peace, and His power. All of which He has freely given you, His child. Child of God, ask what you will of Him and believe! Replace your fear with faith! Replace your fear with His power!

Thought #244

Ps. 139:10: "Even there Your hand will guide me and Your strength will support me."

You may ask, where is there? There is wherever you are. Wherever you are, there is God. If you are His child, He is always right beside you. Won't you take His hand? Lean on His strength to get you through whatever it is you are going through. He loves you and will take care of you. Trust Him, He is worthy! He will never let you down. He will never fail you. He will never leave you to handle it yourself. Trust Him to be what you need Him to be!

Thought #245

Matt. 22:29: "Jesus answered and said to them, 'You are mistaken, not knowing the scriptures nor the power of God.'"

There is only one way to get to know God, and that is to read His Word. We can pray to Him night and day. We can go to church, church functions, gospel concerts, or sit and talk with Christian friends all day long, but until we start looking for Him where He is, we will never get to know the one true God, His promises, His power, or His intentions for us. We cannot have an intimate relationship with someone we do not know. I pray that God fills you with an overwhelming desire to develop a personal relationship with Him. He will not force Himself on you. You can live a life of abundant blessing or abundant struggle. The choice is yours. Which do you prefer and to what lengths will you go to receive the abundance He is willing to pour out on you?

Thought #246

Phil. 4:19: "And this same God who takes care of me will supply all your needs from His glorious riches, which have been given to us in Christ Jesus."

It does not matter what your need is. It does not matter how great or how small, God is able and willing to fill that need. Whether physical, mental, emotional, or spiritual God can and will take care of it. Not because you deserve it, not because you earned it, not because you paid for it with money, works, or even faith. But because He loves His child! Trust His love and let Him handle whatever it is that you are going through. His way is perfect, His way is victorious, His way is the only way!

Thought #247

Prov. 23:7: "For as he thinks in his heart, so is he."

Without resorting to justification, who do you think you are? Is it who God wants you to be? Is it who you want to be? Is it who someone else wants you to be? Is it someone whom God would welcome into His Kingdom with open arms? That is what we all hope for, but if we are honest with ourselves, is that what we would hear? If we took a brutally honest look at our heart and lives, would we hear, "Welcome home, My good and faithful servant?" Or would we hear, "Depart from Me, I know you not"? Are we even brave enough to take that close of a look at our heart? What would happen if we looked through God's eyes? What would we see? Think about it. Ask God to help you see yourself through His eyes.

Thought #248

Dan. 6:23: "The king was overjoyed and ordered that Daniel be lifted from the den. Not a scratch was found on him, for he had trusted in his God."

I love the last sentence of this verse! There is so much hope to be found here. If we but trust in the one true God, we too can come through any storm, struggle, trial, or attack from the enemy without a single scratch! And not just without a scratch, we can come out on top and much wiser! Whatever it is you are going through, know that all you have to do is trust God to bring you through it! God controls everything, even what happens next in your life, if you let Him. Storms, struggles, trials, and attacks come when we don't trust God and take control out of His hands. Stop fighting both ends of the battle! Relinquish control to God and let Him bring you, like Daniel, through it without even a scratch!

Thought #249

First Thess. 5:24: "He who calls you is faithful, who also will do it."

If it is God's will, then it is also His bill. God will make it happen, for He who calls you is faithful. God never calls us to do anything without faithfully keeping His word and enabling us to do it. He will also supply the resources to do whatever He tells you to do. Whatever it is you are facing, whatever He has told you to do, trust in the character of God. It is His nature to be faithful. He will never bring you to anything without equipping you to do what He asks you to do. Be brave, be strong, and remember you can do anything through Christ! Anything!

Thought #250

Eccles. 6:9: "Better is the sight of the eyes than the wandering of desire: this is also vanity and vexation of spirit."

Enjoy what you have rather than desiring what you cannot or do not have. Dreaming or wishing for things or people you cannot have is like chasing the wind, a waste of time! When you sit around wishing your life was different, you miss out on the joy that comes from wholeheartedly living the life you do have. Are you homeless? starving? alone? unloved? No? Then you are rich compared to some. We must learn to rejoice in whatever season we are in. It could be so much worse! Remember, if whatever you wish for was good for you, then God would have already given it to you, for He holds nothing good from us.

Thought #251

Luke 11:10: "For everyone who asks, receives. Everyone who seeks, finds. And to everyone who knocks, the door is opened."

The Kingdom of God and all it holds is not about earning or deserving. It is about believing and receiving. No one can "get good enough" or "do enough" to receive God's good grace. The Bible says, ask believing and you shall receive. Believe with all your heart, mind, and strength! What are you waiting for? Submit to God and receive His abundant support, help, resources, and blessings. God is waiting. Nothing you can ask for is too big for Him!

Thought #252

Prov. 20:24: "A man's steps are of the Lord; how then a can a man understand his own way?"

If you know you are walking the path God put you on, do not waste your time nor His by questioning every step. If you know for certain you are in obedience, go with the flow and understanding will be revealed to you as you follow God's lead. Don't be worried about the results, the Master Planner has already taken care of that. You worrying about it won't help it anyway. However, it could change, limit, or even delay what God wants to do. His timing and vision are perfect. Trust Him, follow his lead, and watch miracles happen!

Thought #253

Isa. 41:13: "For I hold you by your right hand—I, the Lord your God. And I say to you, don't be afraid. I am here to help you."

If you are a child of God, it doesn't matter what you are going through, be it a storm, a disagreement with a friend, looking for a job, or even working on your relationship with God. He is always there holding your hand and guiding you in the right direction. Whatever *it* is, just trust Him to be your guide and to get you through it. Listen for His voice and obey what you hear. He will never take you in the wrong direction. Everything you hear from God is for your profit, even when it profits someone else!

Thought #254

Acts 5:39: "But if it is of God, you cannot overthrow it—lest you even be found to fight against God!"

Many times, we may blame our troubles or storms on the enemy, the world, life, or our flesh, and sometimes that is what it is. But disobedience is truly the biggest cause of all our problems. Once we step out of God's will, we set ourselves up for a battle and ultimately defeat. Disobedience is the first place we should look for the cause of our struggles, storms, and tribulations. God's plan is God's plan. You can fight it, you can run from it, you can even refuse it, but God's plan for you will not change! If, on the other hand, you are not fighting against God, you are fighting beside Him, and while you may be in a battle, the battle has already been won. This is God's promise and He never lies!

Thought #255

Ps. 111:1: "I will praise the Lord with my whole heart."

When I am sick, I will praise the Lord. When I am depressed, I will praise the Lord. When I am at the end of my rope, I will praise the Lord. When I am at the end of my money, I will praise the Lord. When I am in the middle of the darkest night, I will praise the Lord. When I am in the middle of the storm and the waves are over my head, I will praise the Lord. When there is no end in sight, I will praise the Lord. When at the end of my misery, pain, confusion, fear, and worry and God has brought me to the mountain top, I will, again, praise the Lord. He is God, and regardless of what I am going through, He is worthy to be praised! He is faithful and true! He is

God almighty and worthy to be praised! I will praise the Lord, no matter what I think I see on the horizon, or how I might feel, what kind of storm I'm in, or how dark the night may be. He is my God, my Father, my Rock, my Hiding Place. There is nothing He can't or won't do for me! My Lord is worthy to be praised, simply because of who He is.

Thought #256

Heb. 12:14: "Pursue peace with all people, and holiness, without which no one will see the Lord."

What do people see when they look at us Christians? Do they see our drama? Do they see our faith in God? How do they see us react to our storms? Do they see us or our faith in God? Never think the world isn't watching to see if we really believe what we say we believe. Do they see a CHRISTian or a christian? Remember, actions speak louder than words. The world and God watch our actions rather than our words. What are your actions saying about you and what you believe?

Thought #257

Hab. 3:18: "Yet I will rejoice in the Lord! I will be joyful in the God of my salvation."

The verse before this talks about the fig trees having no blossoms, the olive crop failing, the fields lie empty, the flocks dying, and the barns being empty, but Habakkuk says, "Yet I will rejoice." If we can get past our view and our opinion of the situation/storm we are in and just praise God, that's when God truly gets to be God! Praise Him! Praise Him! Praise Him!

If everything else goes wrong, you are still alive and have reason to be joyful! If you are a child of God, regardless of what you think you see, the battle has already been won! Do not trust your human eyes, heart, or reasoning, they are all faulty! Ask God to open your spiritual eyes to see your enemy's defeat!

Thought #258

Jer. 5:22: "'Do you not fear Me?' says the Lord, 'Will you not tremble at My presence, Who have placed the sand as the bound of the sea, by a perpetual decree that it cannot pass beyond it? And though its waves toss to and fro, yet they cannot prevail; though they roar, yet they cannot pass over it.'"

Waves may toss and roar, but they can never pass the boundary the Lord has set. It doesn't matter how big your storms seem, if you are a child of the one true God, bought by the blood of Jesus Christ, then you can rest assured He will protect you. Those waves that come crashing in will never harm you as long as you are trusting God to handle it. It may not seem so, but He has set the boundary, and nothing can pass by it. The storm, regardless how high the waves or how loud the thunder, will not drag you under as long as your trust in Him does not fail. Keep your eyes on Him, your trust in Him and He will bring you through to dry ground.

Thought #259

John 3:16: "For God so loved the world that He gave His only begotten Son, that whoever believe in Him should not perish, but have everlasting life."

God gave a begotten Child to save a yet-to-be-adopted child! What a loving, compassionate thing to do! Could I have done the same? Could you or I choose to let our own child die to save a child that might possibly choose to turn their back on you? Can you imagine the love it takes to even consider something like that? He knew! He knew that *He* would have to pursue us, convince us, draw us, prove Himself to us, yet He gave His most precious Child so that we could have everything Jesus gave up to save us! There are no words to describe the love and appreciation we should feel for this Gift God gave us! I cannot even begin to comprehend what it would take to do this for someone else. I thank God it was not up to me to make that decision! I am sure world would still be lost!

Thought #260

Matt. 6:33: "Seek the Kingdom of God above all else and live righteously and He will give you everything you need."

God does not, will not, and cannot lie. Seek Him in all you do. Trust Him to do what is right for you. No one knows what you need better than He does. He has heard your prayers and He knows your heart. Prayers are deathless, once prayed, they stay in the throne room until answered in God's timing. He is faithful. His love and concern knows no limit. His strength, wisdom, and resolve is unfathomable. He never grows weary in His pursuit, protection, or provision. His love and His will never fails. Whatever you need, He has! Seek Him in all you do and He will be found by you! All your needs will be met in Him.

Thought # 261

Mark 6:50: "For they all saw Him and were troubled. But immediately He talked with them and said to them, 'Be of good cheer! It is I; do not be afraid.'"

God keeps every promise He makes! Don't become discouraged or impatient if what God has promised you has not yet come to pass. Hang on to the promise He made. Remember our timing is not the same as His.

Jesus promised that when we ask in His will and in His name, believing, He will give it to you. However, if you are not ready to receive the fullness of that promise, He may be taking the time to prepare you for it. What a waste it would be if He gave it to you and you squandered it away or even missed it because you were not prepared to live out all the blessings that promise entailed! Wouldn't you rather have to wait it out than to miss out? Do not get discouraged! If you ask His will, in His name and believing, then that Promise has your name on it and you can believe it is coming! Hang on and trust the Promise Maker to deliver it!

Thought #262

Ps. 22:19: "But You, O Lord, do not be far from me; O my Strength, hasten to help me!"

If you belong to God, bought and paid for by the blood of Christ, you are not alone! You are not a victim! Oh yes, we have enemies! The spirits of doubt, fear, loneliness, broken relationships, illness, pain, confusion, loss, bitterness, addiction, anger, pride, and hate are a few of the enemies that try to break us. But we have the ultimate Warrior fighting those battles for us!

If you believe God's Holy Spirit lives inside you, then you have the strength and the power of God! You are not a victim! You cannot be a child of God and a victim. It just doesn't work that way! It is not possible! Claim your victory! Rebuke and refuse those spirits that would have you believe otherwise. They belong to the father of lies! If you are truly a Blood-washed child of God, there is no way to be the enemy's victim. Being a victim is calling God's Word a lie. For I can do anything through Christ who strengthens me!

Thought #263

Rom. 8:37: "Nay, in all these things we are more that conquerors through Him that loved us."

Despite everything, despite everyone, every circumstance, trial, or storm victory is ours through Christ! If you belong to Him, the victory is already yours! There is no maybe, no will be, no waiting! The victory is already ours! If you love God, accepted Jesus Christ as your savior, and believe His God-inspired, man-written Word, then you must have confidence in the promises you read. You must have confidence in the One who promised them. You must believe God is bigger than and has already conquered everything the enemy has or will ever throw in your path. If you believe, if you love, then you must trust! You cannot have one without the other. Through Christ, you are a conqueror! Believe!

Thought #264

Mark 10:52: "And Jesus said to him, 'Go, for your faith has healed you.' Instantly the man could see, and he followed Jesus down the road."

Having faith and being faithful are two different things. Being faithful is showing up every time, which really doesn't take that much effort. However, having faith is much harder for us humans. It's believing and trusting in something or someone we cannot see or control. Jesus said you must really believe and hold no doubt in your heart. This is not something we do willingly or naturally. This is something we must learn through experience. To learn through experience, then we must experience God on His terms. We must develop a relationship with Him in order to experience Him. Seek that relationship and you will find Him and the faith you need to follow Him and receive all He has for you.

Thought #265

Rom. 14:4: "Who art thou that judgest another man's servant? To his own master he standeth or falleth. Yea, he shall be holden up: for God is able to make him stand."

Who am I to judge or condemn anyone! Who are you to judge or condemn anyone? Only God can say who will stand and who will fall. With His help, they will stand and receive His approval. What we see with our human eyes is not what God sees with His eyes. We only see what's on the outside; the Bible says God looks on the inside. We cannot know for sure what's in a person's heart. It is better that we close our eyes and mouth to what we think we see in others. Because regardless of what we see on the outside, we have no way of knowing what God is doing on the inside. What is revealed about our inside if we presume to think we are better or holier than anyone else? Jesus chastised the Pharisees for that exact thing. What would we see if we looked inward with God's eyes? If we look to ourselves with God's eyes, and honestly judge ourselves, we will not have time or inclination to judge another.

Thought #266

Mark 14:38: "Keep watch and pray, so that you will not give into temptation. For the spirit is willing, but the body is weak."

How often do we miss our miracle because we didn't wait long enough? When we pray for things and they don't come when we think they should, the temptation to give up becomes so very strong! How many answered prayers have we missed out on because we didn't keep watch and pray? How important is what you've asked for? Is it important enough to continue to pray until you have the answer? Or will you give in to temptation and give up? Do not listen to the lies of your enemy! Keep watch and pray until you receive!

Thought #267

Rom. 15:4: "For whatever things were written before were written for our learning, that we through the patience and comfort of the scriptures might have hope."

I have found much hope and encouragement in reading my Bible and so can you. To find this hope and encouragement and peace, you must look for it. Read your Bible; all this and more is in there. If you have trouble, as we all do, in the beginning, there are many versions out there that make the reading easier. I started out with a parallel Bible, KJV on one side and NLT on the other. There are many parallel versions out there, pray about it and follow the convictions of your own heart. Some will say one version is superior to another. But remember this, every Bible on every shelf is only a version of the original script.

According to Paul, even in his day, the scriptures had been written long ago. Pray about it, get an answer from above, and obey it. You cannot find hope, encouragement, peace, strength, or a relationship with God if you are not looking for it in the right place. You cannot know God without having a personal relationship with Him. That relationship and everything else you could possibly need is waiting in the scriptures.

Thought #267

Num. 6:24–26: "May the Lord bless you and protect you. May the Lord smile on you and be gracious to you. May the Lord show you His favor and give you peace."

Ask believing and you shall receive! Ask in His name and you shall receive! This is your Father's promise to you. Do not let the enemy lie and say you don't deserve it. If God has said yes, it will be yours. Believe! It is on its way!

Matt. 15:28: "O woman, great is your faith! Let it be to you as you desire."

Thought #268

Ps. 119:73: "Thy hands have made me and fashioned me: give me understanding, that I may learn thy commandments."

(NLT: "You made me; You created me. Now give me the sense to follow Your commands.")

Lord, I know that I am not here by accident. I know that You created then molded me to love You, live for and to serve You. Lord, I ask that You give me wisdom so that I might understand Your commands. Open my eyes to Your activity, open my ears to Your voice, open my heart so that I love others the way You love me. Create a great passion in me for what You would have me do. Father, I trust you and believe in Your purpose for me. Teach me to follow Your commands.

Thought #269

Zech. 4:6: "Then he says to me, 'This is what the Lord says to Zerubbabel: it is not by force nor by strength, but by my Spirit, says the Lord of Heaven's Armies.'"

Rely on the Lord of heaven's army to fight this battle for you. You do not have enough power, strength, or know how to get you through it. But God does. Trust Him, allow Him to carry you through this. His way is always the best way. Sometimes the only way to stand tall and strong is to first fall to our knees. Trust God, He will get you through this!

Thought #270

Ps. 27:14: "Wait on the Lord; be of good courage, and He shall strengthen your heart; wait, I say, on the Lord."

Be strong and take heart and wait for the Lord.

Ever notice how often this verse, in one form or another, shows up in the Bible? Ever wonder why? We live in the most fast-paced time in the history of time. We are always rushing to get to the next "thing."

To us, time is of the essence. For God, time is essential. We are always in a rush to "fix" things. But unlike us, God doesn't want to slap a Band-Aid on something requires delicate surgery! God's way, the best and perfect way, includes deep workings to remove all the impurities in us, even the ones that cannot be seen with the naked eye! Slow down, be strong, be determined, be vigilant, be flexible. Give God the time He wants to do what He wants in you. Resist the temptation to rush, wait on the Lord! What He has in store for you is beyond what your brain can comprehend! Let Him have His time and way in your life. Sit back, relax, and watch what God can and will do for you, in you, and through you.

Thought #271

Prov. 16:28: "A dishonest man spreads strife, and a whisperer separates close friends."

Look what happened when Satan decided to "be friends" with Eve. Not everyone you call friend has your best interests at heart. Some have ulterior motives and don't care how they use you to get what they want. Some just want in your business so they have something to talk about. Some just want you as miserable as they are. When it comes to friends, ask yourself if they talk bad about others to me, will they talk bad about me? The answer is usually, yes! Don't be deceived as Eve was deceived. If you know a person tends to speak ill of others for no reason other than to have something to talk about, they most probably speak the same about you to others. Ask God for discernment, He will give it to you. The Bible encourages us to discern (not judge) the spirits of others. Ask and He will give you discernment.

Promise #272

Prov. 27:19: "As in water face answereth to face, so the heart of man to man."

(NLT: "As a face is reflected in water, so the heart reflects the real person.")

It doesn't matter what face we put on, the heart will always shine through. Sooner or later, the true self comes through! That's why the Bible says, "I will give him a new heart and a new spirit." And to be transformed, not conformed. I pray, dear friend, that the Father create in us both a singleness of heart and mind so that our mouth doesn't say one thing and the life we live say something different. To teach us to love and obey You with our whole heart, soul, mind and strength. You are our only hope, dear Lord. I trust you to do what needs to be done in our lives.

Thought #273

John 14:14: "If ye ask anything in My name, I will do it."

Okay, so you've asked and you've asked and you've asked but nothing has happened. We know the Lord does not lie, but still, you've asked and asked, so what's the problem? He said He would do it, so why hasn't it been done? Why hasn't it been given? The Bible says God searches our hearts, He knows the intent of all our hearts. So to answer the question, "Why didn't I get what I asked for?" maybe we should ask what our motives are. Do I ask this because I need it? Do I ask this because I want it? Do I ask this because everyone else has it? Do we ask out of pain, bitterness, jealousy, or maybe even revenge? Why do I think I need this? What good will it do me in the end? Has this prayer not been answered because God has something better in mind and I'm so hung up on what I want I'm refusing what He is trying to give me?

If we learn to ask the right questions, God will answer. He will never withhold any good thing from His child. Trust Him to do what's best for you.

Thought #274

Mic. 3:8: "But truly I am full of power by the Spirit of the Lord."

Say it with me! But truly I am full of power by the Spirit of the Lord! I am a child of the Almighty God! Nothing can stand against me! Nothing can defeat me! My Lord has given me the power and authority to bind the powers of hell and send it back to whence it came. No devil in hell or on earth can touch me, unless I give it permission. I am protected by the Blood and promise of His word! But truly I am full of power by the Spirit of the Lord.

I refuse defeat! I refuse failure! I refuse, resist, and rebuke the lies and tricks of my sworn enemy! No evil shall prosper against me. I have been claimed by the Commander of heaven's army, and as His child, I will not be defeated! In the name of Christ Jesus, this is my birthright and my inheritance! I will stand on the promise of my God!

Thought #275

Phil. 1:27: "Only let your conduct be worthy of the gospel of Christ."

If we say we are Christians, that we love the Lord, then our lives should line up with the words of our mouth. If it does not, then we live a lie. We've led the world to believe a lie about, not only ourselves, but also about God. What do our words, thoughts, and actions live up to? truth? lies? deception? godliness? holiness? a mixture? Saying we belong to Christ but living any other way than Christ-like is a lie. There is no gray area here. It is either black or white, yes or no. There is no in-between, no mixture. Either we belong or we do not. We each must ask ourselves, what is my conduct worthy of?

We have heard it said, "You can't live like hell and expect to go to heaven." What direction are we headed? What direction are we leading others in by what they see in our lives? Lord, help us, teach us to live worthy to be called by your name!

Thought # 276

Prov. 26:17: "He that passeth by, and meddleth with strife belonging not to him, is like one that taketh a dog by the ears."

It's a pretty sure bet that if we interfere in someone else's drama, whether by invitation or not, it will come back to bite us. As foolish as it is, we usually just step right into the fray. Why, because we are human? Maybe, but this verse leaves no doubt to what God thinks about us getting involved in anything that doesn't directly involve us. Resisting the temptation to get involved is pretty simple. If it's not your toy, don't play with it. If it's not you story, don't tell it. Just because we know about it or have an opinion about it doesn't mean it's a good idea to voice it. It's a pretty sure bet if you pull on that dog's ears, it will end up biting you!

Thought #277

First Cor. 10:21: "Ye cannot drink the cup of the Lord and the cup of the devils: Ye cannot be partakers of the Lord's table, and the table of the devils."

We cannot have what our flesh demands *and* what God wants to give us. We cannot bow down to our flesh and raise up our hands for God's blessings. We must choose one or the other. God will not bless those who do not love Him above everything else in their lives. Why should He? I read something a while back that said we cannot live with the devil and expect God to pay the rent. Yet we continue to do as we please and still expect God to give us everything we ask for.

According to the Bible, it doesn't work that way. If you want all God has to give, then you must step up and get a backbone. We must reply to our flesh, our enemy, our friend, our devil with a loud and resounding *No!* and become the woman/man, husband/wife, mother/father that God wants us to be. We will not experience God's abundant favor until we do. We cannot expect God to carry us when all we do is slap His hands away every time He tries to pick us up. We cannot serve two gods.

The Bible says we will either chose One or the other. Which do you choose?

Thought #278

Rom. 12:9: "Let love be without hypocrisy. Abhor what is evil. Cling to what is good."

Before we condemn that person for the sin we think we see in their lives, we must remember two things. First, we ourselves are not without sin, and yes, it is as bad as theirs! Second, Jesus Himself commanded us to love one another. He did not cherry-pick reasons to love or not love. Let love be without hypocrisy! We are not called to love or accept the sin we think we see, but we do have to love the person. Jesus said to abhor or hate the sin but to cling to what is good or, in this case, the person. The sin and the person are not the same. We must learn to separate the two.

How would you feel if God's love for you were determined by the sin He sees in your life? Go ahead, hate the sin, but pray for and love the person with your whole heart. And yes, even that person that hurt you. Remember, Jesus didn't cherry-pick, and neither can we!

Thought #279

Prov. 9:17: "Stolen water is sweet; food eaten in secret is delicious."

Be careful what you do and say here on earth! Remember, the verse what is done in darkness will be brought to light. If it causes you to sin, it is not a blessing for God. If it causes pain or suffering to a brother or sister, it is not a blessing from God. Those ill-gotten gains, regardless of what it is or how you obtained it, is not a blessing from God. And it is not God's will. We might get away with things here on earth, but once we step into the pure light of God, it will be revealed. He has knowledge of it before we even think to do it. And with conviction, He tries to persuade us to not do it. So never doubt that when we come face-to-face with God, He will judge accordingly and we will answer for it. Is what we want worth what will come?

Thought #280

Ps. 56:3–4: "Whenever I am afraid I will trust in You… In God I have put my trust; I will not fear, what can flesh do to me?"

I praise God for what He has promised with this verse. When you have lived with any kind of overwhelming fear for any length of time, you too will praise Him, if you let Him take that fear away! If we trust God the way we say we do, then why should we be afraid? Sometimes, as in my case, fear can become so consuming we can't seem to get free of it. But if we trust God, He can and will set us free. Our biggest and worse enemy is ourselves and the flesh we wear! And that is usually what causes our strongest storms. God has promised over and over again that we can be free of all bondage, even fear, which causes depression, anxiety, bitterness, and broken relationships. All we have to do is trust Him and even our own flesh has no hold on us. Trust Him and watch the chains fall away!

Thought #281

Prov. 16:2: "All man's ways seem innocent to him, but motives are weighed by the Lord."

It's not what a person does that determines his motives, but why he does it. God knows our heart and He knows why we do the things we do. Man may see and applaud the work of our hands, but God sees the work of our heart and blesses it accordingly. Be sure of your motives. Good work pleases God more if our motives are pure. The Bible says if we work to be seen or applauded by man, then that is all we will get. But works done in secret and with pure motives will delight the Lord. Do we work for man's applause or God's delight? Be obedient and remember whose opinion matters most.

Thought #282

Exod. 33:14: "The Lord replied, 'I will personally go with you, Moses, and I will give you rest—everything will be fine for you.'"

A child of God is never alone! He will never give you more than you and He can handle. He will never let you fight a battle alone. He will never let you climb any mountain too high for you and He to conquer. He will never let you navigate any storm or rough sea without His calming presence. He will never give you more responsibility than you are ready for. Close your eyes and breathe! You are not alone! He is right beside you guiding you, listen for His voice, and He will give you rest. If you will allow Him access to whatever it is, He will bring peace to anything and everything you could possibly go through. Trust Him, listen for His voice, He is there waiting to take over. You are not alone!

Thought #283

Ps. 103:3: "Who forgives all your sins and heals all your diseases."

Our God is a God who heals. He heals the broken! He heals broken bodies, broken lives, broken minds, broken hearts, and broken relationships. There is nothing He can't heal. We have not because we ask not. Ask and believe He can do what you ask. Believe God can do what He says He can do. He does not lie. Ask, believe, and trust Him to heal what is broken in your life. He is waiting for you to bring it to Him. Once we have truly put the broken thing in His hands, it becomes His responsibility and He is obliged to heal it. Sit back, be patient, and be vigilant, and you will be able to see the healing begin. Don't get worried if it doesn't look the way you expect it to. God's way is not our way, it is the best way!

Thought #284

Ps. 37:5, 7: "Commit everything you do to the Lord. Trust Him, and He will help you… Be still in the presence of the Lord and wait patiently for Him to act."

Don't worry about what other people say or do. Do not compare yourself, your family, your life, your heart, your desires, or your ministry to anyone else's. Whatever God has told you to do, do it! Do what you know to do and trust God handle the rest. The worst thing we can possibly do is compare ourselves or anything we do to what we think we see in someone else. God has chosen you specifically to do what He has asked you to do. You are the best person to do it. Unless directed otherwise by God, you need only Him to help you. Commit everything to the Lord and He will help you. If you are unsure of anything, all you have to do is pray, be still and wait patiently for the Lord to act. Trust Him and His love for you. He will not guide you wrong. Listen for His voice, move when He says move, and let Him handle the outcome!

Thought #285

Prov. 10:19: "When words are many, sin is not absent…but he who holds his tongue is wise."

The more we talk, the more we expose the thoughts within us. Sooner or later, the sinful thoughts are revealed. It doesn't matter how we dress, where we go to church, where we live, what we drive, how much money we have, or who we think we are. Sooner or later, our words and actions reveal to a watching world who we really are! What do your words and actions say about you? What truth do they reveal? Are they Christ-like? Are they worldly? Or are they fueled by your flesh? What does your words and actions tell the world about you? If our words and actions do not line up with God's word, it would be wise to just hold our tongue.

Thought #286

Prov. 3:5: "Trust in the Lord with all your heart and lean not on your own understanding."

There are times when we pray and God gives answers, and there are times when we pray and God gives peace. Sometimes we pray and cannot see or hear God at all. We cannot know the ways of God, but we know that if we belong to Him, He hears us, and He will answer us. Just because you don't see, hear, or feel an immediate response does not mean He has forsaken you or even answered with a no. It very well could mean only that you are not ready for the answer, you aren't in a position to receive it, or the answer didn't come in the form you were expecting. God always hears His children's prayers

and delights in answering them. However, He will not give you anything that will end up harming you. He will not give you anything
you aren't ready for. He will, however, give you exactly what you
need, when you need it. He is always working things out for your
good and His glory. Trust Him! Be patient, He heard you and your
answer is on the way. Your job is to position yourself to receive it.

Thought #287

Rom. 12:18: "If it is possible, as much as depends on you, live peace-
ably with all men."

Jehovah-Shalom, the Lord is our peace. When you've obeyed
the Lord and done all you can do to reconcile with that one person,
when you've come to the end of your rope and you know you've done
everything the Lord has told you to do, when you finally realize you
can't fix it, there comes a time we must brush the dust from our feet
and move on. Do not move on with anger in your heart. Make peace
in your heart and love with all your heart. Love them and leave them
to the Lord. Trust Him to handle the situation. Sometimes we have
to make peace with ourselves to be able to live in peace with others.

Thought #288

Rom. 12:9: "Let love be without hypocrisy."

Dear friends, I know I have used this verse in the pages of
this book, but I feel in my spirit that we cannot stress this scripture
enough! We cannot say we love someone and at the same time condemn then for whatever perceived sin we think we see in their lives.
Who are we to name their sin? Who are we to presume it is our job to
point their sin out when we sometimes refuse to see our own?

Can I tell you something? One, they already know what they
are doing. Two, if we worry about what's in our own lives, we will
not have time to worry about what's in someone else's life. Three, if
God shows you something is someone else's life, first make sure it was

God, then pray and pray hard before you decide to go to that person. Do not speak before you know for sure what God wants to say to that person through you. Four, regardless of what you see or think you see, love that person with your whole heart. That person will know if you speak in love or condemnation. We do not have to condone the sin to be able to love that person. We all have sin in our lives! Before speaking, we all have to check attitudes of superiority at the door. Remember, Jesus Himself warns against throwing rocks.

Thought #289

Second Chron. 20:15: "For the battle is not yours, but God's."

Nothing you can do will bring your situation victory the way God can. He is Jehovah-Jireh! He sees past your wants and provides what you need. He is Jehovah-Nissi, He will fight for you with more strength than you'll ever be able to muster. When you have nothing left to give, He is just getting started.

He is Jehovah-Shalom, He is peace unimaginable. His peace He will freely give you. His peace ends all turmoil! There is nothing He cannot bring His peace too.

He is Jehovah-Shammah, He is always there. He will never leave you nor forsake you. These are His promises to His redeemed child. Reach out, grab hold of the Promise! He is waiting on you! What are you waiting for?

Thought #290

Ps. 16:8: "I know the Lord is always with me. I will not be shaken, for He is right beside me."

Be courageous! Do not give up! God is our only hope. Trust Him in everything. He will not let you fall if you just hang on to Him. He is all you need. Whatever has come against you will not shake you if you believe in His promise to you. If God be for you, then no man can be against you. If you are in a spiritual battle, God will protect you. There is nothing to fear with Him by your side. Not even the devil himself can cross the Bloodline. You have nothing to fear, but fear itself. Fear is a lie and a trick from Satan to get you to doubt your Lord and Savior. God has promised to never leave you and God cannot and will not lie. Trust Him to get you through!

Thought #291

Luke 18:27: "He replied, 'What is impossible for people is possible with God.'"

It doesn't matter what you are facing, it doesn't matter how high that mountain looks, it doesn't matter how far from God your loved one is, it doesn't matter how deep the claws of addiction have sunk into your family. It doesn't matter what the doctor says, it doesn't matter what the judge says.

There is nothing too big or too small for God. If you will lay it in His hands, He will handle it for you. Give Him total control and watch what happens. You've got nothing to lose! God already knows what you are going through, He knows what you are facing, and He knows the remedy. He longs for you to come to Him and lay it at His feet. Trust Him, He is all you need. He is waiting to be your everything!

Thought #292

First Tim. 4:14: "Do not neglect the gift that is in you."

By God's own word, we are all called. We are each given a gift. This gift is specifically for us and given to us that the Lord may use it through us to help others. Do not neglect nor quench the gift. Let it grow and mature as you grow and mature in the Lord. Who you are depends on what gift you are given; never doubt that you have a gift. Reflect on who you are, not what you can do. God works through this gift, you do not. So what you can do has no bearing on what He can and will do. He only needs a willing vessel; He will do the rest.

Pray that God reveal and guide you as you learn to be His vessel. He will fill you with everything you need to operate in the gift He gave you. If He tells you to do something, do it. The outcome is His responsibility, not yours. Your responsibility is to love Him, seek Him, and obey Him. He will handle the rest. He will not ask you to do something He has not equipped you to do. Trust Him. He will use you if you allow it.

Thought #293

Isa. 7:11: "Ask a sign for yourself from the Lord your God; ask it either in the depth or in the height above."

Jehovah-Shammah, the Lord is there. He is always with us, in all places, in all circumstances! God is always available and always present. God's response is always, "I am with you." All you have to do is reach out to Him. He will answer you in whatever you ask. Open your mouth and ask; open your ears and your heart and your hands to receive. Ask believing with your whole heart and you shall receive. This is His promise to all His redeemed children. No father will deny his children any good thing. Your heavenly Father is bound to do the same and more. As much as your earthly father may love you, it dims in comparison to the depth your heavenly Father loves you. Ask believing with your whole heart and watch what happens.

Thought #294

Second Tim. 2:13: "If we are faithless, He remains faithful; He cannot deny Himself."

Thank you, Lord, for being who You are! Even when we have no faith left, He is faithful! He will never leave you to handle your trials alone. Our Lord has promised to always be there, even in the middle of your storm! It is His nature to always be faithful and He cannot go against His nature.

God is God, and regardless of what we face, He will always be there to take care of His children. He cannot deny Himself or who He is. He is love. He is mercy. He is grace. He is compassion, patience, peace, protection, and provision. He is perfection.

When you trust Him, all that He is will manifest itself in your life. There is nothing He won't do for you, except give you things that will harm you. Everything He gives or withholds is for your good. Let God be God in your life and reap the benefits of His nature and character. This, dear friend, is my prayer for you.

Thought #295

Job 1:7: "The Lord said to Satan, 'Where have you come from?' Satan answered the Lord, 'From roaming through the earth, going back and forth in it.'"

Satan answered the Lord, even Satan answers to the Lord! He has won the victory against Satan and holds all the power! As soon as God opens His mouth, Satan has no choice but to obey. Your protection and your provision are covered by this Power. When Jesus left this physical world, He sent the One who would give us the power to rebuke and resist Satan and all his lies and tricks. The Power lives inside you; access it by submitting to God and letting Him handle the devil's ungodly agenda. When God speaks, all the demons in hell tremble. This is the power that lies at your fingers. Submit and be empowered to do all things through Christ. "For with God nothing shall be impossible!" Claim this promise and His power as your own.

Thought #296

Second Sam. 22:29–30: "O Lord, you are my lamp. The Lord lights up my darkness. In your strength I can crush an army; with my God I can scale any wall."

With God as your source of strength, you can do anything. What looks impossible becomes possible. The mountain that looks insurmountable becomes a molehill in your rearview mirror. When you are at your lowest point and there's no way out, God will be there. He will light you a path through the darkest night. He will calm the angriest storm with just one word. He will bring peace to whatever battle you find yourself in. You are backed up by the God of heaven's army and no enemy on earth or in hell can touch you. He can and will do that everyone says can't be done. He has the last word in every situation. He is your confident hope. He will always be there to see you through. Trust Him. He is the only one that can do what you need done!

Thought #297

Second Cor. 3:16: "Nevertheless when it shall turn to the Lord, the veil is taken away."

Isn't that the most wonderful statement you've ever read? All we have to do is turn to the Lord, and the veil is taken away so that we can see and reflect on the glory of God. Once the veil is lifted and we can gain a better understanding of who God truly is, we can get to know Him and strive to be more like Him. It says where the Spirit of God is, there is freedom. Freedom from our sin, past, anger, bitterness, pain, jealousy. Confusion, illness, loneliness, fear, worry, addiction, stress, freedom from everything that is not from God. Aren't you ready for freedom from the struggle, storms, trials, and suffering? Turn to God and let Him free you from every chain that binds you from receiving your freedom, peace, and joy! He is waiting on you! What are you waiting on?

Thought #298

Job 23:10: "But He knows the way I take; When He has tested me, I shall come forth as gold."

God knew before you were born where you would be right now, and He made provisions for this season in your life. He has not left you to deal with this alone. However, what you now decide to do will determine how you will come out on the other side. Will you trust

Him to bring you through the fire? Will you trust Him to remove all the dross and impurities from your life?

We may not always know what His plan is, we may not always see, hear, or even feel Him, but He always knows where we are. And what He has planned is more than you can wrap your mind around. Let Him bring you through the darkness to the fire so that you can come forth as gold. He will never take you anywhere He doesn't go with you. You are never alone! In the darkness, the fire or on the mountaintop, He will always be right beside you.

Thought #299

Titus 1:16: "They profess to know God, but in works they deny Him."

Do our words and works match up? If we profess to be Christian, then our actions should be Christ-like. This is what the world looks for when looking to Christians. If we say we are Christian but our lives do not line up with God's word, we lie. If we say we are Christian but our love for another is tainted by the sin we perceive in their lives, we lie. If we claim to be Christ-like but live in bitterness, anger, pain, jealousy, unforgiveness, pride, indifference, etc., we lie. Our lips can say anything, but as the world watches, it is how we live our lives that determines who we are in their eyes. If we profess we know God, Love, or live for Him but our lives don't line up with who He is, then we have sinned against God by lying about Him. We cannot say one thing and live another and still be qualified to call ourselves reborn children of God. Speak and live truth, let your no be no and your yes be yes.

Thought #300

Heb. 3:7–8: "Therefore, as the Holy Spirit says, "Today, if you hear His voice, do not harden your heart as in the rebellion in the day of trial in the wilderness."

God gives warnings only while there is still hope. God never warns when there is no hope left. There is no need, it is already too late. If you get a warning or a call, heed it! It very well may be your last chance. Do not tarry too long. You never know what day is your last day. You never know what breath is your last breath. You never know what call will be the last call you hear. Do not take chances with your life and certainly not with where you will spend eternity. Do not harden your heart or stiffen your neck against what God would give you. Listen quietly, every little whisper in the storm counts. Every flicker of light in the darkness means something. He will not leave you stranded without warning. Listen, watch, and obey.

Thought #301

Deut. 28:8: "The Lord will command the blessing on you in your storehouses and in all to which you set your hand, and He will bless you in the land which the Lord your God is giving you."

This is His heart's desire, to bless you and to enrich your life with His presence, His guidance, His will, and His way. The Bible says in Psalms 121 that He is your keeper and shall neither slumber nor sleep. Your help comes from Him. All you have to do is repent and confess Him as your personal savior, live a life pleasing to Him, and ask for what you need. Talk to Him, listen to Him, and obey. In return, He promises to bless you in your storehouse. He will bless all that you set your hand to. He will bless you in all that He has given you. Everything you have is from the Lord. Let Him bless and multiply everything He has already given you. Let Him bless you in your relationships. Let Him bless you in your home. Let Him bless you in your job. Let Him bless you with things yet to come. Cry out to Him, He will hear you, He will not deny you, He will answer you! This is His promise!

Thought #302

Second Cor. 10:4: "We use God's mighty weapons, not worldly weapons, to knock down strongholds of human reasoning and to destroy false arguments."

We are not alone! We do not have to fight every battle by ourselves! We have the one true God at our side. There is nothing beyond His control! If you are a Blood-bought, Blood-covered child of God, there is nothing you can't do! There is nothing He wouldn't do for you! Put on your armor and use every weapon the God of heaven's armies has put at your disposal. He is faithful to those that love Him. This battle has already been won! Claim it and thank Him for the victory.

Thought #303

Matt. 23:26–28: "Blind Pharisee! First cleanse the inside of the cup and the dish, that the outside of them may be clean, also. Woe to you, scribes and Pharisees, hypocrites! For you are like white-washed tombs which indeed appear beautiful outwardly, but inside are full of dead men's bones and all uncleanness. Even so you also outwardly appear righteous to men, but inside you are full of hypocrisy and lawlessness."

Holiness is not a look; it's a way of life. Holy is from the inside out. Not the other way around. Unlike man, God looks at the heart. Anyone, including Satan himself, can dress the part. God doesn't look at the closet, unless it's your prayer closet! So never judge a book by its cover. I praise God for not judging me by man's standards! I would have never made it past the first couple months after salvation!

My "inside" started changing immediately but my "outside" took a lot longer to catch up! And believe me, dressing the part is the easy part. Learning to listen and obey was a little harder. It took a while to realize God wanted to be more than a wish list or a bank account. He wants a relationship. He wants our love, our trust, our confidence. He wants your heart, not your clothes.

Thought #304

Exod. 20:3: "Thou shalt have no other gods before Me."

This includes yourself, your husband, your children, your boy/girlfriend, you job, your church, your ministry, your bank account, your entertainment, your addiction, your hurt, your bitterness, your anger, or whomever may have caused you pain. Whatever you spend the most time thinking about is your god. Choose this day whom you will follow. You cannot have two gods before you. Will you choose God the Father or His enemy? Because if you choose anything or anyone other than God, you have chosen His enemy. Do not let your flesh or someone else's flesh become His enemy.

Thought #305

John 1:5: "The Light shines in the darkness and the darkness can never extinguish it."

In the movie *A Bug's Life*, several of the bugs were shouting to another bug, "Don't go into the light!" It was cute and it was funny, but think about it, you know that when we get saved, we all have those friends who try to persuade us in just that way. But if you are tired of being beat down, hurt, angry, bitter, disappointed, confused, sad, or just plain tired, then I am shouting to you, "GO INTO THE LIGHT!" I promise there is no better place to be than standing in the circle of God's light! Let Him shine His light on you and extinguish all the darkness in your life. The definition of darkness is the partial or total absence of light. You don't have to be a lost or unredeemed sinner to be sitting in partial or total darkness. Sometimes life just happens and we step away from the light. Whether you are lost and need salvation or just got lost along life's rocky old road, my prayer for you is that you allow God to shine His light into your life, trust Him. There is no greater love than the Father's love for His child. He will bring peace to whatever storm, trial, or dark place you are traveling through. Go into the Light, there is no safer place!

Thought #306

Mic. 7:8: "Do not rejoice over me, my enemy; when I fall, I will rise. When I sit in darkness, the Lord will be a light to me."

No enemy can defeat me, my faith, nor my God! Even when my faith runs low, my God never runs out. My Lord is my light, my strength, my joy, my comfort, and my faith. My God is my everything! He never fails me! If I stumble, He corrects me. If I get tired, He carries me. If sorrows come, He will bring joy. If chaos rules, He will bring peace. There is nothing He won't do for me. There is no other like my Lord. There never has been and there never will be! What a wonderful, faithful, and trustworthy God we serve.

Thought #307

Josh. 23:14: "And you know in all your hearts and in all your souls that not one thing has failed of all the good things which the Lord your God spoke concerning you. All have come to pass for you; not one of them has failed."

Not one promise that God has made to you has ever failed. God cannot lie! It might not have looked like what you thought it should, but if He promised, then the promise has already been fulfilled. All you have to do is accept His promise. When God promises us something, it's up to us whether we accept it or not. What He promises is always true and right! It is yours for the taking. Just because it's wrapped in a different package than you expected doesn't mean it's not what you asked for. When God speaks, adjust your life to be filled with *all* God's promise. No one can do it for you! He knows what you need better than you do. Step up, accept your promise regardless of what it looks like!

Thought #308

Eph. 4:1: "I, therefore, the prisoner of the Lord, beseech you to walk worthy of the calling with which you were called."

God knew you before you were born, that means He put a calling on your life before you were born. He has called you to be His. He has called you to love Him and be like Him. Can the way you are living right now be called worthy of that calling? I challenge you to take an honest look at your life, ask the Lord to reveal what He sees when He looks into your heart, mind, thoughts, actions, and motives. Ask Him to reveal where you might have stepped away from the life He has called you to live. Be brave, ask Him to help you correct the areas He reveals. He is eager to help you realign your life with His will and His vision for you. Trust Him to make you complete and wholeheartedly His and true to your calling.

Thought #309

Ps. 23:3: "He restores my soul; He leads me in the paths of righteousness for His name's sake."

He knows your every need! You are never alone! You never have to call God into your situation. As a reborn child of God, He is already there. He goes before you, He walks beside you, He comes behind you. He protects you and will never leave you. He knows that in our walk with Him we can become exhausted from trials, temptation, burdens, and even our ministry can become a heavy cross to bear. But He is always there. He is always waiting to strengthen us, comfort us, bring peace to whatever storm that may be raging in our lives. Don't give up! Ask Him to restore you. He promises that all you have to do is ask believing and it shall be done. He loves you more than you can imagine! He will answer this prayer!

Thought #310

Second Sam. 22:29: "O Lord, you are my lamp. You light up my darkness."

Have you ever felt lost? Not lost as in you didn't know where you were. But lost as in you didn't know what to do or where to turn. Lost as in you've done all you know to do and nothing can get you out of what you are in. Lost as in you are at the end of your rope with no strength left to hold on. Friend, let me tell you, you are not alone! Everything is not lost! God is waiting to carry this load for you. God is waiting to bring hope and light back into your life. Call out to Him and let Him bring light, peace, comfort, and answers back into your world. He is waiting just for you! Call out to Him. He will answer you!

Thought #311

Ps. 11:5: "The Lord tests the righteous."

We can't change what the future holds, but we can change our reaction to it. How we respond to God's tests reveals our spiritual progress. When these tests come is our chance to prove what we know to be true about God. If we will turn to Him, trust Him, spend time with Him in prayer, and in His Word, He will sustain us. It doesn't matter what the future holds; this is His promise to us. Believe His promise, trust in His love for you. He will get you through the test.

Thought #312

First Thess. 5:7: "Pray without ceasing."

Never stop praying! It doesn't matter what your head tells you, your thoughts are not God's thoughts! It doesn't matter what your eyes see, God sees way beyond what you are able to see. It doesn't matter what your ears hear; unless it's God's voice telling you what comes next, you can't trust what you think you hear. It doesn't matter what others tell you, they are not God. God is the only one that knows the end of the story. Trust Him and never stop praying, even if it feels as though the prayers are only going ceiling high. Remember, you can't fix it, but God can! Give it to Him, trust Him, pray, and rejoice knowing that God can and will handle every situation in your life. Nothing is too big or too small. Trust Him, He's got you!

Thought #313

John 9:3: "'It was not because of his sin or his parent's sin,' Jesus answered. 'This happened so that the power of God could be seen in him.'"

Have you ever made a decision or a series of decisions so bad that it put you in a place you never wanted to find yourself? Then wonder how you got there? God gave us free will, and sometimes that free will puts us in places we never thought we'd be. However, God loves us enough to take the bad and turn it around for our good, if we let Him. Everything He does is for us, is for our good and so that His love, power, and glory can be seen by a watching world. No matter how bad I messed up, and believe me, it was bad more times than I would like to admit. He loved me enough to lift me out of the mess I got myself into. All I had to do was give it to Him, believe in Him, and trust Him to do what was best for me. That's all you have to do! Let God show you His love, mercy, grace, compassion, glory, and power. Let the power of God be seen in your life! You will never regret giving it to God.

Thought #314

Heb. 10:13: "It is a fearful thing to fall into the hands of the living God."

The best thing you will ever do for yourself and your loved ones is to put everything you are into the hands of God. Yes, it can be scary. Yes, your life will be forever changed. Yes, there are things and people you will have to give up. But I promise it's nothing compared to what you will receive! All the things we hold so dear and cling to the hardest is nothing but trash compared to the blessings God has in store for us. Think about it! Is what you have right now so amazing that it can't get any better? Would you be reading this if it were? Don't wait until you "fall into" the hands of God at the end of your life. If you are standing on the edge of the cliff of decision, I encourage you to jump straight into the waiting arms of the one true living God. He has promises and blessing beyond your comprehension waiting for you! Take that leap of faith and watch what happens! Fall in love with God and watch what His love for you will do!

Thought # 315

John 15:17: "These things I command you, that you love one another."

So simple! Love one another. It doesn't say love each other as long as that person agrees with you, or as long as that person is loveable or pretty or nice or believes the same as you. It says love one another. That means the good, the bad, the ugly, the hated, the mean, the sweet, the everything! Though it does not say it, it means love each other, regardless.

John 13:15 says, "I have given you an example to follow. Do as I have done to you." I pray that the Lord will teach each of us to love others the way He has loved us. There is no other way! Is it fair to expect God to love us unconditionally if we refuse to love others the same way? He has given us an example to follow, therefore, we have no excuse!

Thought #316

Acts 11:17: "If therefore God gave them the same gift as He gave us when we believed on the Lord Jesus Christ, who was I that I could withstand God."

If God loves everyone the same, treats everyone the same, protects everyone the same, gives gifts to in the same manner, who are we to stand in His way? I wonder how many times we limit God by getting in His way? How many times do our "gentle" prayers for ourselves or our loved ones limit what God would really like to do in us and through us? What miracles would we see if we took the gloves off and start praying prayers that shake the gates of heaven? How many demons would flee at the sound of your voice calling out to the Commander of heaven's armies? How many souls would be saved if we would pray, "Whatever it takes, Lord!" and mean it? Can you even imagine it? Be brave, be strong, pray those "whatever it takes" prayers, and watch heaven come down to earth for you! Believe and it will happen! That is God's promise to you!

Thought #317

Acts 10:15: "But the voice spoke again: 'Do not call something unclean if God has made it clean.'"

We are all so quick to name the sin we think we see in other people's lives, never once stopping to realize unless God opened our spiritual eyes to what He is doing in that person's life all we can see is what our human eyes want to see. Unless we know without doubt that God has prompted us to speak on it, then we should hold our tongue. We too have sinned against God and have no place to judge or condemn another. I pray that God would close our human eyes and open our spiritual eyes, that He teach us to see and love beyond what we think we see. To love them regardless of what we think we see. And remember He loved us even at our worst.

Thought #318

Matt. 5:18: "I tell you the truth until heaven and earth disappear not even the smallest detail of God's law will disappear until its purpose is achieved."

Jesus did not come to change any of God's commandments. He came to achieve their purpose. So my question to myself is, if He didn't come to change them, why do we think we have the right to change them? The Bible does not say obey the ones you like and forget or change the ones that don't suit you. I'm guessing everyone is guilty of cherry-picking when it comes to obeying the scriptures.

I have certainly done my share in my time. However, that doesn't make it right.

John 14:15 says, "If you love me, you will keep my commandments." Unfortunately, it doesn't say some or most. In fact, it's pretty clear. If we love Him, we will keep all His commandments. If we don't, then we must not love Him the way we say we do. I am so thankful that repentance will save me from my disobedience and a contrite heart will help me strive to obey His commandments.

Thought #319

Luke 12:31: "But seek the Kingdom of God, and all these things will be added to you."

What is it that you want? Do you like where your life has led you? Do you know where you would be right now if you had stopped doing things your way when God first told you what He wanted you to do. Do you realize you can change everything? All it takes is a little talk with God and then obey what He tells you. Will it be easy? Probably not. Will you like what He tells you? Again, probably not. But will you prosper from it? Most definitely! God promises all these things will be added to you! What are you waiting on? To see what other things will happen if you don't? Or would you rather have everything God promised you? What are you waiting for? Put God first in your life and all good things will be added unto you!

Thought #320

James 2:10: "Whoever shall keep the whole law, and yet stumble in one point, he is guilty of all."

So according to this, it does not matter if we keep all God's commandments except that one little tiny one that's not even one of the big ten. We are as guilty as if we have broken them all. But we point our finger at someone else's sin, talk about their sin, condemn them for their sin, all the while justifying our own sin. Which, of course, is laughable because nowhere in the Bible does it give rank and file on sin. In God's eyes sin is sin. My gossiping is as big as the murderer or pedophile. My overeating is the same as the addict's addiction. With God there is no justification, sin is sin. If we do not judge our own sin as God would then who are we to judge another. God shows no partiality. We will all be judged the same as the murderer, the pedophile, the drug addict, the liar, the smoker, the drunk and the gossips. We are all the same! Guilty!

Thought #321

Josh. 10:8: "'Do not be afraid of them,' the Lord said to Joshua, 'For I have given you victory over them. Not a single one of them will be able to stand up to you.'"

It does not matter who "them" may be. If you, like Joshua, are a child of God who loves and obeys Him, He will defend you. It does not matter who, what, when, or where the attack comes from He will give us victory over "them." Not a single one of "them" will be able to stand up to you. So forget your fear! God's got this, and He will not let His loving, obedient, born-again child down! He will always be there. Trust Him to see you through!

Thought #322

Matt. 6:7–8: "Ask, and it will be given to you; seek and you shall find; knock and it shall be opened to you. For everyone who asks, receives, and he who seeks, finds, and he who knocks, it will be opened."

So if this is a promise of God to believers, then why aren't all our prayers being answered? Is it because we ask without believing? Is it because we ask amiss? Is it because the timing isn't right? Or is it because of our own inability to see that we have not done our part to be ready for the answer?

I think a lot of time this is most probably the case. For example, if I ask God for a job, but never go out and look for one, I have not done my part. If I ask God for a new vehicle, but never bother to start saving for the down payment, I have not done my part. If I ask God for a child, but have not put any effort into creating a marriage or home ready for that child, I have not done my part. If I ask God for a husband but I have not done what God says do to prepare myself to be a godly wife, then I have not done my part. Or I've asked for a healing but have no intention of changing the bad habits that may have contributed to illness, then I have not done my part.

I think we sometimes ask God for things hoping that they will be miraculously dropped into our laps without any effort on our part. Yes, God can do that in the blink of an eye, but why should He? When you pray, ask yourself, have I done my part? What is my part? Then ask God to reveal to you what you need to do to prepare for the blessing you've asked for. Then obey what He tells you! Then expect your answer, it will come!

Thought #323

First Tim. 2:1: "Therefore I exhort first of all that supplications, prayers, intercessions and giving of thanks be made for all men."

You noticed the word *all*, right? It is easy to pray for our loved ones. It is even reasonably easy to pray for our not so loved ones. However, this calls for us to pray, intercede, and give thanks for all! What?! Seriously? Even that person that said that thing, even that person that did that thing? Even the mean, hateful, spiteful person that no one likes? Yep! Even that person! All means all!

I pray that regardless who or what we face, God will give us a heart to love like He does. I pray that He reminds us of this verse anytime we are tempted to disobey it. Help us to remember to pray and give thanks to and for the loved, the unloved, and the unlovable. These things I ask for you and for me. For if we don't have love for others, we do not have love for the Father.

Thought #324

Acts 2:25: "For David says concerning Him: I foresaw the Lord always before my face, for He is at my right hand, that I not be shaken."

He is right beside me! When I need strength, He is there. When I need peace, He is there. When I need comfort, He is there. It matters not what you go through, it matters not what you need, as a reborn child of God, He is right beside you to see you through, He will always give you what you need. Be brave, as bad as it may seem, He is always right there beside you! Let Him be who and what you need. Let Him love you through it. He will not fail you if you just trust Him.

Thought #325

Deut. 23:5: "Nevertheless the Lord your God would not listen to Balaam, but the Lord your God turned the curse into a blessing for you, because the Lord your God loves you."

Don't worry about the situation, how big the mess is, how loud that storm roars, or how many come against you. God can and will turn anything into a blessing if we let Him. He is our Savior, Redeemer, Protector, Comforter, and our Healer. He wants nothing more than to be our everything! Love and obey Him and watch Him turn those curses into blessings. And remember, nothing is set in stone until God sets it there! Nothing is finished until God says it is finished. Forget what you see or hear and trust what God knows. He knew the ending before you begin the beginning. Walk by faith, even when you cannot see!

Thought #326

Second Cor. 5:7: "We walk by faith, not by sight."

Sight is limited, faith is not. Can you imagine having to live by only what you can see? Can you imagine having to live in the middle of a storm forever because that's all you can see? Can you imagine fighting the enemy day after day after day because we can see no end in sight? Can you imagine never having the strength, courage, faith, and wisdom to know that what's in front of you is only temporary? What a horrible existence that would be! I will live by faith *knowing* that what's in front of me will not limit me. I will live by faith and move forward out of the storm. I will live by faith *knowing* the battle I fight has already been won. I will live by faith knowing victory is mine! I will live by faith *knowing* that what I see is not what my reward is. I will live by faith *even* when I cannot see the other side. And so can you!

Thought #327

Josh. 7:13: "You cannot stand before your enemies until you take away the accursed thing from among you."

Have you ever wondered why your life is a continuous struggle? Have you ever asked yourself why does it seem like you are always under attack? Nothing goes right? No light at the end of your tunnel? That maybe, even God has forsaken you? Where is God, where are those blessings He promised? I want to encourage you to do what God told Israel to do. Look for that deep hidden thing (sin?) that keeps blocking those blessings. We cannot stand before our enemies nor receive the blessings God has promised us if that "accursed thing is blocking what God wants to give us." That accursed thing might not be considered very big or it might be hidden from you. Search deep, be honest with yourself and with God. Ask Him to reveal the reason you are in the place you are in. Then do whatever it takes to remove or change the thing that has your blessings blocked. You are not alone in this. He loves you more than you can imagine. He will help you get rid of it.

Thought #328

Deut. 4:35: "To you it was shown, that you might know that the Lord Himself is God; there is none other besides Him."

Open your eyes to the truth. Open your ears to His voice. Open your heart and accept there is no other way. God's way is the only way. If you chose not to follow it, you will be miserable. The King of kings, Lord God Almighty Himself has chosen your path. Walk it and see what He has in store for you. Step beyond it and find out what misery truly is. Let God bless you beyond your wildest dreams. He loves you and will take care of everything you could possibly need.

Thought #329

Isa. 30:29: "You shall have a song as in the night...and gladness of heart."

Be not dismayed whate'er betide. God will take care of you. Beneath His wings of love abide. God will take care of you. What better way to chase the enemy away than to walk around with a song in your heart? He cannot drag you down as long as the praises of God ring out in your heart and head! There is no room left for the enemy to dwell as long as you keep a song in your heart. There is no torment so great that can shut down or overcome the praises of God. There is no darkness that can defeat the praises of God.

My pastor's grandfather used to shout out during worship, "Sing, children, sing!" He has been gone several years now, but I can still hear his sweet voice encouraging us to lift our voices in praise! He was in his eighties when he passed and six minutes before taking his last breath his granddaughter recorded him thanking everyone for their love and prayers. I don't believe he went a day without a song in his heart. I want to encourage you to remember to "sing, children, sing." When the night is the darkest, *sing*! When the waves are over your head, *sing*! When your heart is breaking, *sing*! When there's no light at the end of the tunnel, *sing*! When anxiety and depression threaten to overtake you, *sing*! Will you always feel like it? Probably not, but if you sing, you will defeat whatever it is that the enemy uses against you. So again, I say, "Sing, children, sing!"

Thought #330

Rom. 2:11: "For there is no partiality with God."

No one is more loved by God than you are! No one! It doesn't matter what you've done in your past. You are as loved as the greatest of saints! It doesn't matter that you are not loved by man, you are very much loved by God. God thought you worthy of His death. He loved you so much He died for you! With His last breath, He prayed for you. At this very moment, He is interceding for you. God loves you. Trust Him! He will take care of you!

Thought #331

Second Tim. 2:16, 23–24: "Avoid worthless, foolish talk that only leads to godless behavior." Verse 23 and 24: "Again I say, don't get involved in foolish, ignorant arguments that only starts fights." A servant of the Lord *must not* quarrel but must be kind to everyone, be able to teach and be patient with difficult people.

Paul thought this important enough to mention twice, so then it must be imperative, right? As I read and thought about this the question that rose up in my spirit was, what must unbelievers, the lost, the unchurched, think of God's children when they see us acting in this manner? Why would they want to be one of His children if that's what they see in us? How are we different and set apart if we act no different than the rest of the world? We are called to be an example by the way we live and act toward each other. Pray the Lord will reveal the example we are setting. Help us see what He and the world sees in us then to help us correct anything that grieves His Spirit or brings dishonor to His name. Teach us to be a good example and to close our mouth unless what we speak comes from Him. Help us to be kind and patient with everyone! Yes, even that person that just crossed your mind.

Thought #332

Ps. 27:14: "Wait patiently for the lord. Be brave and courageous. Yes, wait patiently for the Lord."

Shhhh, be still and wait! We are always in such a hurry to get where we are going, but nothing lasting happens in an instant. We live in a microwave world, so we are used to everything happening at the snap of our fingers. But I can bet that many of those snap decisions have more than not turned out to be wrong, even disastrous. The grass is not always greener on the other side! Be patient and know that God is getting you ready for something bigger than you are equipped to handle at this moment. If you jump in too soon, it could cause ruin. Be brave, be patient, it is coming!

Thought #333

John 14:13: "And whatever you ask in My name, that I will do, that the Father may be glorified in the Son."

Ever had one of those AHA! Or, Duh! Moments? Yep, that's me right now! How selfish has my thinking and my thanking been? Until this very moment, it never occurred to me that the answers to my prayers have been for anything other than my good! Absolutely, my answered prayers benefit me and those I prayed for, but that's not why they were answered! I've read and claimed this verse many times, but until this very moment, the last part of this verse never really hit home. My prayers are not answered just for me! They are answered to bring glory to the One who answers them. When God is glorified, everyone benefits. Forgive me for being blinded by my selfishness! To God be the glory for every answered prayer! There have been so many! Forgive me, Lord, for my childish thinking. Thank you, Lord, for opening my eyes and revealing truth to me. To God be the glory for every yes and no answer!

Thought #334

Heb. 4:16: "So let us come boldly to the throne of our gracious God. There we will receive His mercy, and we will find grace to help us when we need it most."

When I read the words "come boldly," I see in my mind and action of walking boldly to God and telling Him what I need. But in truth, by the time I realize I can't do it on my own, by the time I realize I need God to get through it, I am rarely on my feet. By then, I am usually dragging myself to the feet of God, begging His forgiveness and help. Come boldly simply means to come without fear. He beckons us to come without fear of being turned away. He waits for us! Regardless of how hardheaded, stubborn, and rebellious we are, He waits for us with unconditional love, mercy, grace, and compassion. So come or drag yourself boldly, without fear to the throne of your gracious, loving, compassionate Father and receive the help you need.

Thought #335

Acts 17:24: "God, who made the world and everything in it, since He is the Lord of heaven and earth, does not dwell in temples made with hands."

This is what we are taught, and as children of God, this is what we believe. He spoke the universe into existence! He said, "Let there be," and it happened! Yet we have trouble believing He can handle our puny little storm. We let worry and fear become bigger than the Creator of life! If we believe He did all this, if we believe Jesus said simply, peace, be still, then there is no reason for you to believe that He cannot bring peace to your situation. Believe, have faith! God can and will handle it, if you just give it to Him. He is faithful! You never have to worry when what you need is in His hands.

Thought # 336

Acts 27:25: "So take courage! For I believe God, it will be just as He said."

You can take courage that whatever you are going though is not too big for God. Don't let your doubt, fear, worry, pain, anger, jealousy, or bitterness limit what God wants to do in your life. Jesus told Paul in 26:14, "It is useless to fight against My will." Aren't you tired of fighting? Give up the fight and let God handle the situation. Don't you believe He can do it? There is nothing your God won't do for you! *He* is your protection, your provision, your rock, your hiding place, your deliverer, and your redeemer. He died to save you from hell. Don't you think He can handle this? Or is it that you believe He can but wonder if He will? Why wouldn't He? He promises He will! He does not lie, therefore, what are you waiting on? Trust Him, He loves you and has no desire to see you suffer. Lay it at His feet and walk away. He will take care of it and the solution He presents will fix it permanently. Be brave and believe He's got this!

Thought #337

Phil. 2:12: "Work out your own salvation with fear and trembling."

Once we are saved, no one can tell us how, specifically, to stay on the path that God lays out before us. However, Deut. 26:17, 18, says, "Today you have proclaimed the Lord to be your God, and that you will walk in His ways and keep His statutes, His commandments, and His judgements, and that you will obey His voice. Also today, the Lord has proclaimed you to be His special people, just as He promised you, that you should keep all His commandments."

This is how we stay on the path that He has laid out for each of us. Open your Bible, the map, directions are clearly printed inside. Follow this map and you will never get lost.

Thought #338

Ps. 33:4: "For the Word of the Lord holds true, and we can trust everything He does."

Everything God does on our behalf is for our good. When we pray and ask God for something, we have usually already decided how it should come about. Then we become frustrated because it didn't go the way we expected it to go. Then we assume God did not hear or did not answer our prayer. Never doubt, if you are His child, He most definitely heard you.

The Bible says His thoughts and ways are higher than ours. God sees the end from the beginning and He knows the best path to get there. When you give something to God for Him to handle, don't limit Him with your idea of how it should go. Give Him free reign to do what must be done and trust that the outcome will be in your best interest. God loves you and will do what is best for you. He is not interested in giving half measures. Trust Him and His vison for your life.

Thought #339

Prov. 8:17: "I love those who love Me and those who seek Me diligently will find Me."

If we aren't willing to give more than a few minutes to God in prayer, then we certainly cannot expect more than that from Him. A fly-by-night, off-the-cuff, two-second prayer will be heard and answered by God. But have we any right to expect anything other than the same kind of answer? If you truly need something that only God can give you, then you should be willing to put the time in to make sure you get what you need. Targeted, consistent, unceasing, and fervent prayer will get you what you need and more. Seek diligently and you will receive.

Thought # 340

First Pet. 3:9: "Don't repay evil for evil. Don't retaliate with insult when people insult you. Instead pay them back with blessing. That is what God called you to do and He will bless you for it."

I speak from experience when I tell you the hardest thing you will ever do is pray blessings on the person that hurt you. But this is what God has asked us to do. Don't do it for the blessings God promises you, do it because you know in your heart it is the right thing to do. Do it out of the love that God has called us to have for one another. Do it in obedience to the One who gave us life, The One who forgave and wiped away every hurtful thing you did to Him. Do it, not because they deserve it, but because without it, you cannot get forgiven. Do it because if you don't let it go, it will fester into anger, bitterness, and pride. Do it before these spirits take hold and define who you are. Remember, you are a child of God, and if you submit to Him resisting the enemy's evil plan against you becomes a matter of telling him to leave you alone and he has no choice but to do just that. Do it because that's exactly what Jesus did for you.

Thought #341

Rom. 4:21: "He was fully convinced that God is able to do whatever He promises."

Verse 18 says even when there was no reason for hope, Abraham kept hoping. Even though He knew his and Sarah's bodies were as good as dead, his faith did not weaken. Sweet child of God, no matter how dark the night may seem, if God made you a promise, it will come to pass. Hold on and believe, dear child, it is coming! Though weeping may endure for a night, joy comes in the morning. That's God's promise to you. Hold on, have faith! If God said it, God will make it happen. He is more than able to do what He says. All you have to do is hold on and believe!

Thought #342

Prov. 9:10: "The fear of the Lord is the beginning of wisdom, and the knowledge of the Holy One is understanding."

You have to know someone to have an intimate relationship with them. Just knowing about them or who they are will not give you that intimate knowledge and understanding of them. Just having knowledge does not give understanding. We say we know who God is, we accepted Him as our Lord and Master and that we follow Him. But do we really? Do we know Him, respect Him, and honor Him with our words, actions, and lives? Are we truly living as His word instructs us to? Or are we living the way that seems right to us and our flesh?

Prov. 16:25 says, "There is a way that seems right to a man but in the end leads to death." Without knowing and understanding God intimately, we cannot have the wisdom it takes to live, think, and speak the way He would have us do. Without an intimate relationship with God, we will say and do things that bring shame to His name, respect His name, and seek to know Him, love Him, and obey Him with all your heart, mind, strength, and spirit. Get to know His character, His nature, and His Word. Then and only then will you have wisdom, knowledge, understanding, and discernment.

Thought #343

Rev. 3:16: "But since you are like lukewarm water, neither hot nor cold, I will spit you out of my mouth."

Friend, I pray the Father will create a passion in you for Him like that of an all-consuming raging fire. That He teach you to keep that fire burning in your spirit for all the things that are dear to our Lord's heart. I pray He gives you ears to hear what He has to say to you, eyes to see what He sees in you and what He would have you see in others, and a heart to love everyone as unconditionally as He loves you. I pray that He gives you a heart full of love, mercy, compassion, patience, and words of encouragement. I pray He teaches you to live holy as He is holy and blameless so that others can find no fault in you. That the world sees Him in you. In Jesus's name, I pray this for you. Amen.

Thought #344

Gen. 18:14: "Is anything too hard for the Lord? I will return about this time next year, and Sarah will have a child."

If God can bless and use a dried-up, worn-out old woman like Sarah to create a nation, what could He do through you? If God is God, the creator of heaven and earth, who spoke the world into being, do you not think He can and will speak life into whatever you are going through? Do you not think He is able to do whatever it is you need done? Come to Him as His child and ask what you will in His name, believing and it shall be yours. Your responsibility is to love, trust, and obey Him. Let Him bless you. Let Him use you as He did Sarah. If He is your God and you are His child, He will bless you as much as you will allow Him to. You can sit around and laugh or scoff at God's promises as Sarah did in the beginning or you can gather your courage and believe He is who He says He is and will do what He said He would do. The choice is yours.

Thought #345

Ps. 134:2: "Lift up holy hands in prayer, and praise the Lord."

It does not matter where you are in life. You can be in the deepest, darkest valley or high on the mountaintop. You are not alone! If you are His child, God sees you, hears you, and is waiting to help you. The Bible says ask, believing, and it shall be yours. If you believe the Bible to be the true Word of God, then you have no reason to fear! Raise your holy hands, thank and praise your heavenly Father for what He has done or what He is about to do. All you have to do is love Him, keep His commandments and believe! Whatever you need—peace, joy, comfort, mercy, grace, courage, strength, wisdom, knowledge, healing, forgiveness, deliverance—it can all be yours, it's up to you. Start thanking Him now and watch what happens! Do not be discouraged, He hears you!

Thought #346

Matt. 28:18: "All authority has been given to Me in heaven and on earth."

God gave Jesus the ability, the power, and the freedom of all heaven and earth to do God's will. Then Jesus said, "You will do even greater things." Where are these greater things? Where is the evidence of greater things in our lives? The very Son of God, not only said this, He also went away so that *He* could send the One who would enable us to do these greater things. Where is our faith? He cannot lie, so then, the problem must lie with us? Lord, help us in our unbelief! Help us to grow our faith in You and Your word that we may do these greater things. Forgive us for not taking You at Your word. Help us, Lord, to do what You would have us do. What we do next will reveal what we believe about our Lord.

Thought #347

Luke 10:17: "Then the seventy returned with joy, saying, 'Lord even the demons are subject to us in Your name.'"

Why are you struggling? What are you fighting? Who are you fighting? The Bible says, even the demons are subject to us in His name. We have been given authority over all the power of the enemy and nothing shall hurt us (Lk. 10:19). Yet we struggle, wrestle, fight, and even argue with the enemy! Why?! We have the authority to say, "Be gone," and that's exactly what he must do! Nowhere does it say we must argue, wrestle, or fight with the enemy.

We don't' even have to fight temptation! If we recognize it for what it is, then all we have to do is say, "Be gone," and that too must flee. Whatever or whoever is attacking you, tell it or them to be gone in Christ Jesus's name and move on. Resist the temptation to look over your shoulder to see if it's still there. Say what you believe and believe what you say. You have the authority to live in peace through Jesus Christ! Use the authority He gave you and do not look back. You either believe His promise or you do not. It's a choice, make it and live free!

Thought #348

Gen. 24:40: "He responded, 'The Lord, in whose presence I have lived, will send His angel with you and will make your mission successful.'"

If you are a child of God, bought by the blood of Jesus Christ. If you are living in obedience as His child and He gives you something to do, do it! Whatever it is, however crazy it might sound, you have no reason to worry! He will not send you to do something He will not equip you to do. And He will not send you to do it alone! If you do this in obedience to Him, He will ensure your success! Have no fear, if God has spoken and you have obeyed, it will be done! God Himself will ensure it! Be brave, step out, and answer His call. You have nothing to fear in obedience!

Thought #349

Second Cor. 9:8: "And God is able to make every grace overflow to you, so that in every way, always having everything you need, you may excel in every good work."

When you seek to obey the Lord, He will make sure you have everything you need to do exactly what He asked you to do. So don't be afraid, step out, knowing His grace surrounds you and will supply your every need. You will never out give or use up God's abundance in your life. He will never send you out without giving you every resource you need to do the job He sent you to do. You may think you can't do it, or that you are unworthy. But let me tell you this. If he called you to it, then He has called you worthy. Trust Him, He's got you in this. To quote one of my favorite preachers, "If it's God's will, then it's God's bill." And He is never late on His payments. It doesn't matter if you've got this, He does!

Thought #350

Rom. 8:24–25: "We are given this hope when we are saved. If we already have something, we don't need to hope for it. But if we look forward to something we don't yet have, we must wait patiently and confidently."

Be quiet, be still, be patient, it is coming! You know what it is. You've asked for it over and over again. God has heard and answered. Be still, be patient, be confident, your answer is on the way. Look forward to it, expect it, and rejoice for it. Even though you don't see it right away, immediately begin to thank Him for it. Have no doubt, it is on its way! Your job is to stay obedient. Do what you know to do and let God handle the timing. Be ready to receive the answer, regardless of the form or timing. God's will and timing is perfect. He will use it to bless you beyond your imagination, if you will allow it. Get ready! It's coming!

Thought # 351

First Cor. 1:30: "You are in Christ Jesus who has become for us wisdom from God—that is our righteousness, holiness and redemption."

Without Jesus, there is no redemption, no holiness, no righteousness. We cannot have nor find any of these on our own. Without being reborn into the family of God, we will never have what He wants to give us. We must have Jesus in our heart and life consistently to live redeemed, righteous, and holy. He came so we could have all this and more. Be reborn and let Jesus birth something new in your life. You will be forever changed by what He does for you. Even "backsliders" can't go back to exactly what they were before accepting Christ. We can always go back to living in all out sin, but once Jesus has touched your life, you will never be the same. Your heart and mind will have been awakened to Truth and there's no going back from that. Accept what God has for you and learn to live life more abundantly. Things you never thought possible will become not just possible but will become fact! Once you see, feel, and taste all that's waiting for you, you'll never want to go back to what you used to be! Jesus didn't come to make you better. He came to make you new!

Thought #352

Ps. 101:5: "Whoever secretly slanders his neighbor, him I will destroy; the one who had a haughty look and a proud heart, him I will not endure."

Do you know the Lord has your back, even when you know nothing about it? If you are His child, He will protect you, even from gossipers and evil speakers. Though it hurts to know someone would do such a thing, don't worry about what Ms./Mr. So-and-So said about you. God heard it first and He promises to handle it. God's got it; all you have to do is be still and know that He is God. Look inside yourself to the peace that has already been put there by the Prince of Peace. Let the God of heaven's army fight that fight for you. He will bring you out of the battle unscathed if you be quite and watch. Trust Him and His promise.

Thought #353

Heb. 10:36: "Patient endurance is what you need now, so that you will continue to do God's will. Then you will receive all that He has promised you."

It is in our nature to be impatient, to think what we want should be given now rather than later. It is even our nature to childishly demand to have it now. But God says to be patient, continue to do His will and you will receive what He has promised. My question is, how important is this thing you were promised? How bad do you want or need this promise to be fulfilled? Bad enough to wait on God's perfect timing? Or will you jump ahead of God in your impatience and mess things up? God knows what you need and the perfect time to give it to you. Be patient so that His promise is filled to perfection. Resist the urge to rush things. Stay out of His way and let God be God.

Thought #354

Matt. 6:14–15: "If you forgive those who sin against you, your heavenly Father will forgive you. But if you refuse to forgive others, your heavenly Father will not forgive you."

Jesus said that the measure by which you forgive others will be how you are forgiven by Him. Forgiveness is a choice, but God allows no exceptions when it comes to forgiveness. It must be complete forgiveness. Would you want God to forgive you the same way you are presently forgiving others? We must learn to forgive other the same way God forgives us. We all have broken the Father's heart in one way or another. But He loved us enough to forgive us every time. He held nothing back from us. Pray that He will create in you a forgiving heart. Actually forgiving someone is never easy for our human hearts. But with God's help, we can do it.

Thought #355

Luke 18:21: "Death and life are in the power of the tongue."

We must always be careful what we say, who we say it about, and who we say it to. Remember what we say or repeat gets repeated with our name added to it. What you say or what we repeat says more about us than the person or situation we are speaking about. The more important thing to remember is that God heard what was said and who it was said to. Regardless of our justification, God knows our true motives and will judge us on what *He* knows to be true about us.

Speak truth, speak life, speak freedom! If it's not your story, if it doesn't directly concern you, do not speak at all! The world and other Christians know the truth from the words of our mouth and the actions of our life. Do not let the devil or others trick or manipulate you into having to answer to God for what you said or did, that by God, will be judged ungodly. Gossip and lies continue with a mouth that repeats and dies with the mouth that stays shut. We are judged or rewarded as the case may be. Which will you be? Judged or rewarded? Think before you speak! What will what you say do to your testimony? What comes from our mouth is what we become known for. How and by what do you wish to be known for? Will you be judged or rewarded?

Thought #356

Prov. 11:9: "The hypocrite with his mouth destroys his neighbor, but through knowledge the righteous will be delivered."

With their words, the godless destroy their friends, but knowledge will rescue the righteous (NLT). How many times has someone tried to destroy you or your reputation with words? How many times have our own careless words worked to bring down a brother or sister? We have all failed, we have all been guilty of this. But here's the catch, the more we talk carelessly or spitefully against one another the more damage we do to ourselves. The more we gossip or spread, "well, I heard it this way," or, "so-and-so said that," the more death we speak on others. And the thing we never think about is while we are doing this to someone else we are also killing our own reputation.

Each time we open our mouth to speak death on another, our own testimony as a Christian takes a hit. How many hits does it take to ruin your own reputation and testimony? Let us not be hypocrites! Through knowledge of God's Word, His will, His nature, His character, and our own obedience, we can be delivered of our natural instinct to run down our fellow man.

Think before you speak, think about what your words will ultimately do to yourself.

First Thess. 5:15: "See that no one renders evil for evil to anyone, but always pursue what is good both for yourself and for all." The Bible says, "the tongue can bring death or life; those who love to talk will reap the consequences." Be careful of the consequences you reap.

Thought #357

Prov. 26:20: "Where there is no wood, the fire goes out; And where there is no talebearer strife ceases."

You ever notice that gossip is like a fire? It starts out as a small hate-filled ember burning hotly in someone's heart that ignites into a small flame as soon as it leaves the heart by way of the lips. Then spreads, growing and consuming more and more space as it is fueled by more and more lips. Soon it's burning like a raging wildfire consuming lives and testimonies. Be careful to stay out of the path of the wildfire, it will consume you and your reputation. Refuse to spread the fire. It will go out as soon as the wood has been removed from the path. Refuse to be covered by the smut, smoke, and stink that is always left behind when the fire has burned out. Refuse to be part of the devastation that gossip leaves behind. Let not the fire damage your vessel or consume your testimony as a Christian. Be the godly water that puts out the ungodly fire of gossip.

Thought #358

First John 3:18: "My little children, let us not love in word, neither in tongue; but in deed."

One version says, "Dear children, let's not merely say that we love each other; let us show the truth by our actions." First, let me remind all of us that we can dislike, disapprove, or even hate the actions of someone. But under no circumstances are we as Christians allowed to not love someone. Even if that person is the most unlovable person in the world. Even if that person has done the unspeakable to us. The Bible says, if we do not love one another, then the love of the Father is not in us. We must learn to separate the person we are called to love from the action or actions we dislike. Learn to love them as God loves us. Learn to see them, love them, and treat them as God sees, loves, and treats you. Do not fall into the temptation of seeing only the outside. Ask God to open your eyes, ears, and heart to what He wants you to see.

Thought #359

Ps. 96:8: "Give to the Lord the glory due His name."

What do you have that the Lord did not give you? If not for the Lord, what would you have? If not for the Lord, you would not exist because the world would not exist! Think of the balance God created just to make the sun rise every morning. And that was the easy part! Think of the intricacy of your brain telling your lungs to draw in air! God put so much love and thought into creating us, yet we doubt His love, mercy, grace, kindness, and compassion for us.

As His child, we can ask *anything*, He will hear us and He will answer us. There is no doubt with Him! He is our only hope! Whatever you need, He has! Whatever you need, He will supply. If you are His child, He will not let you do without. He has supplied every need you ever had. He will supply every need you will ever have. So give God the glory and honor He deserves! Count your blessings and thank Him for each one. Without Him, you would have nothing. Without Him, you would be nothing, literally!

Ps. 96:4: "For the Lord is great and greatly to be praised!"

Thought #360

Second Cor. 10:17: "As the scriptures say, If you want to boast, boast only in the Lord."

Without Him, we would not be who we are. Without Him, we would not have what we have. Without Him, we would not be able to do what we do. *Everything* comes from God. Our obedience to Him determines what we get from Him. Your obedience determines your blessings. It is written that God can and will give you everything you need. Are you willing to give as much to Him? God has never failed to be there for me. God has never failed to answer every prayer I've ever prayed. Have I failed Him? Oh yes, many times. But I am His child, and He knows my true heart. He knows my every thought. He even knows what motivates some of those thoughts and He loves me anyway. I am forgiven because I seek repentance for those things which hurts His heart. But I am loved unconditionally not because of who I am, but because of who He is. He is always there waiting for you. No one will ever love you the way He loves you. His mercy, grace, and compassion is unlimited. Take what He offers, you will never regret it.

Though #361

Gal. 4:7: "Now you are no longer slaves but God's own child. And since you are His child, God has made you His heir through Jesus Christ."

As God's heir, you inherit all that He has, all that He is! You have the power of God living inside you. There is no reason to live in bondage. There is no reason to live in defeat. There is no reason to live in sorrow, guilt, pain, anger, bitterness, hate, or jealousy! All of this and more has been defeated by the power of God through His son Jesus Christ. God's power has conquered it all! And if you are a child of God, you have that power living in you! Freedom is yours for the taking! Nothing can stop you. You can be a victim or victor. The choice is yours!

Thought #362

Eph. 5:6–7: "Let no one deceive you with empty words, for because of these things the wrath of God comes upon the sons of disobedience. Therefore do not be partakers with them."

Do not be fooled by those that try to excuse sin. The Bible is very clear on this! In our hearts and in the hearts of the justifiers, we know that sin is sin regardless of the age we live in or the justification our imagination can come up with. God does not rank sin, therefore to God, all sin is the same. If you have questions about what anyone tells you, all you have to do is go to God, His word, and/or your pastor. God will never speak or do anything contrary to His word. If what you hear, see, or want goes against His word, then it is not for you. Do not be deceived either by your flesh or your enemy. Understand, anyone that tells you or leads you to go against God's word is your enemy. Do not be partakers with them or you could very well be partakers of the same consequences they will suffer. Resist the temptation to let the wrong things slide just to fit in. If you are a child of God, you were not paid for with Christ's precious blood just so you could fit in. You are called to stand apart and be a godly example. Do not be fooled by empty words, go to God's word for truth!

Thought #362

John 8:31–32: "Then Jesus said, 'If you abide in My Word, you are My disciples indeed. And you shall know the truth and the truth shall make you free.'"

When you are a child of God, He will reveal all truth to you and that truth will free you, if you believe. Truth is found in His Word and that truth enables you to be free from fear, doubt, confusion, anger, hate, bitterness, addiction, depression, anxiety, pain, pride, rebellion, stubbornness, and whatever else that has you in bondage. Truth can and will break every chain you, the world, and the enemy has managed to wrap around you. Whatever mess you're in, Truth will rescue you and set you on a new path. Truth will give you a new heart, a new mind, and a new life. Truth will bring wisdom, knowledge, understanding, and discernment to every thought you have, every word you speak, every decision you must make. All you have to do is ask and believe. Don't wait hoping it will come on its own! Seek it! Believe it! It's there for the taking!

Thought #364

Gal. 3:27: "For as many of you as were baptized into Christ have put on Christ."

The Bible tells us to put on and wear the full armor of God. This is to protect us from the world, the enemy, and yes, even ourselves. But what about the putting on of Christ? The putting on of Christ does not necessarily mean your clothes, which by the way at some point does play in this, but we won't go into that here. In this case, it means that we should be clothed as Christ the Person. It means the world should see Him when they look at us. Can the world tell who we belong to by the way we speak, act, and live? Or do we wear Christ like a winter coat that we can take off when it gets too heavy or too hot? It may seem an odd concept, but if we "wear" Christ like a second skin, the world would know not only who we belong to, but also, who we spend most of our time with. Our lips would never have to declare who we are, it would be evident! If we have been baptized into Christ then His Spirit lives in us, it is up to us to let Christ shine through us!

Thought #365

Something to Think About

The Bible teaches us our relationship with God is the only thing that comes before our husband. Now before anyone gets upset about this, I want you to think about it. As Christian women who say we follow the Word, we must ask ourselves, is the one true God the only god we put before our husbands? What comes first in your life? children? job? self? parents? family? friends? your feelings? If it is anything other than God Almighty, we are living contrary to God's word. By putting anything, except God, before our husbands, we are committing sin. Never allow your family or your friends to come between you and your spouse. Shield your marriage! Let no seed of division be planted in your marriage. Be the godly wife God meant for you to be. Protect your husband's position, image, and reputation.

Mark 10:9 says, "What God has joined together, let no one separate." Do not let your feelings, your children, your parents, your friends come before your husband. These things and people will not always be there for you at the end of your life, but if you tend your marriage like a starving farmer tends his crops, you will always have your husband's love either to the end of your life or the end of his.

I am not saying everything will be perfect, but you do not have to let the world in on what's not perfect. Keep your private business, private! In no way am I advocating staying in a marriage where there is violence. But if you want the marriage God planned for you before you were even born, then follow God's Word to the letter so that even if it doesn't work out, God will find you blameless. Put God at the top of the ladder, then your husband on the second rung, and everything else will fall into place.

I pray that God will speak to your heart in ways that are clear as glass. I pray that you will have the strength to accept and obey what you hear from Him. I pray God blesses you in all areas and that you take those blessings and bless others! In Jesus's name, I pray, trust, and believe! Amen.

ABOUT THE AUTHOR

Betty Lambert is a lifelong resident of south Mississippi. She and her husband, Mark, have been married for thirty-eight years. They are both active members at Vernal Full Gospel Church. Betty has held several jobs in the past, but the two dearest to her heart were as reading tutor at her local elementary school and Wounded Warrior liaison for the Mississippi National Guard. However, when the Lord told her it was time to put her husband first—both boys were grown with families of their own—she gave up her job and started traveling with Mark, who works with subcontracting companies doing maintenance and repairs at different power plants across the United States. Betty knew many years ago there is a book in her heart waiting to be written. After much prayer and prodding from the Lord, this is the one He chose for her to write. It is her hope, dear reader, that God speaks to you through it.

CPSIA information can be obtained
at www.ICGtesting.com
Printed in the USA
LVHW041348130120
643422LV00003B/105/P

9 781098 012526